KU-354-770

25p

CAMBRIDGESHIRE
LIBRARIES
WITHDRAWN
FROM STOCK

THE LIFE AND DEATH OF DORIS ARCHER

Doris Archer died peacefully in her sleep, sitting in her favourite armchair at Glebe Cottage, Ambridge, in October 1980. But Gwen Berryman, the woman who had acted Doris for the full thirty years of her radio life, was still very much alive and preparing for a well-earned retirement in Torquay. Now Gwen Berryman has written the story of her own life, revealing at last just where her own personality stopped and Doris Archer's took over. As well as chronicling her own story, Gwen charts the ups and downs of *The Archers*, drawing on her own recollections and sense of humour to bring to life those memorable decades.

THE LIFE AND DEATH OF DORIS ARCHER

Gwen Berryman

A Lythway Book

CHIVERS PRESS
BATH

First published 1981
by
Eyre Methuen Ltd
This Large Print edition published by
Chivers Press
by arrangement with Eyre Methuen Ltd
1982

ISBN 0 85119 821 X

Copyright © 1981 Gwen Berryman

British Library Cataloguing in Publication Data

Berryman, Gwen
  The life and death of Doris Archer.
  —Large print ed.—(A Lythway book)
  1. Berryman, Gwen   2. Radio broadcasters
  —Great Britain—Biography
  791.44'028'0924   PN199/.4.B/

  ISBN 0–85119–821–X

CAMBRIDGESHIRE
LIBRARIES

ACKNOWLEDGEMENTS

Grateful acknowledgement is made to Sidgwick and Jackson Ltd for permission to quote from *The Archers, A Slice of My Life* by Godfrey Baseley.

To all those who have
performed
written and
produced
The Archers

and to the millions who
have listened.

AUTHOR'S NOTE

As an actress rather than an author, I am very conscious of the probability of failing my readers. I hope, therefore, that those of you now reading this disclaimer are not as yet committed to spending money on buying the book. Before you put your hand in your pocket, let me warn you that this is in no sense an attempt to document the history of The Archers, nor do I offer any scandalous revelations about what went on behind closed doors. If either is what you seek, I have now saved you some money. You see, all I offer is my personal recollection of almost thirty years' acting in a programme that has become part of the English landscape. I offer no insights, only personal views. I have, however, enjoyed all those years and I hope you will get some pleasure out of reading about them. If you do, perhaps you will join me in thanking: Jock Gallagher, for helping me to gather my scattered wits and edit them into publishable form; my brother Trevor and nephew Christopher, for helping to sort through a lifetime's memorabilia; Tony Shryane and Norman Painting, for reading the manuscript and crossing my t's and dotting my i's; and Sue Marshall, for her monumental efforts in deciphering the scribble and converting it into a polished document.

THE LIFE AND DEATH OF
DORIS ARCHER

CHAPTER ONE

One of the main reasons that finally helped me decide to write about my experiences was a strongly-felt determination to make it clear that there was never any confusion in *my* mind about where Doris Archer ended and Gwen Berryman began. You see, over the years hundreds of newspaper reporters and magazine writers have created for me the image of a nice-but-simple soul whose own frail personality had been somewhat swamped by the scriptwriters' fantasies. I've never done anything to correct matters because, as an actress, I was always flattered that anyone should write anything about me, and the BBC always said the stories were very good publicity for the programme. My autobiography seemed, however, the very place to set the record straight. Here I can say exactly what *I* want. So here and now I should say that Doris Archer is dead. And here and now I should explain how clever I have been in keeping fact and fiction separate for almost thirty years; how the part in the Archers has been just another role, albeit a plum one, that helped to pay the rent. But now when it comes to it, I cannot say any of that. You see, in sifting through a long lifetime's memories, I began to realize that those reporters and writers might not have been wrong after all. I had never had any doubt about how much of Gwen Berryman had gone into the late Doris Archer, but I was really surprised at how much of Doris had crept into my personality. I found that I wasn't going through one lifetime's experiences, but ·two. The division between fact and fiction has been so stretched since my first performance in 1951 that it is now extremely fuzzy in most instances and in others has disappeared completely.

From that, you can perhaps begin to imagine what it was like for me when the BBC finally decided that Doris was to die.

I knew it was coming. It was my own health that had made it necessary. After many years of crippling arthritis and then two awful strokes, I had told the BBC I did not want to go on making the long journey from my home in Torquay to the studios in Birmingham, where the programme is recorded. My doctor had told me that I should not even think about going back to work and reminded me that at seventy-three I was well beyond the normal age of retirement. The BBC bosses were very nice about it all. They told me not to rush anything but to just wait and see if I changed my mind when I was feeling better. Of course, I did not change my mind and they were genuinely reluctant when they finally accepted my retirement. I honestly think they did not want to lose me from the programme. I had ever such nice letters saying how much I would be missed and how much they appreciated all I had done for the The Archers. One of the senior men even came to see me in Torquay. He was the one who, several years earlier, had promised me that if I ever had to give up playing Doris, the part would not be offered to anyone else. This was always very important to me because it was usual to re-cast (there have, for example, been three different actors playing Dan over the years) and I felt it was a great compliment that they believed that no one could follow me. During our conversation in the nursing home, that promise came up and he reassured me that it still stood. While it escaped me at the time, he explained that the inevitable outcome was that Doris would have to die; after all, she was too old (over eighty) to be written out of the script in any other way.

What exactly happened after that I do not know. I was not at all well at the time. The frustration of not being able to talk properly, because of the second stroke, had really got on top of me and nothing much was registering with me. I have since been told that when anyone tried to explain that Doris Archer was going to die on such and such a date, I got very upset and gave the impression that I thought it was me that they were talking about rather than the character. I do remember there was a lot of fuss from the newspapers and I can recall a television camera crew being in my room taking pictures, but I did not really know what it was all about. I don't think I even cared.

When it finally did get through to me that Doris was to die on the programme one Monday evening, I felt really dreadful. I have since seen in the newspapers of the time that I had been advised not to listen by my brother, Trevor, by my doctor, by the matron of the nursing home and by the BBC. Well, I do not know if I actually was given all that advice, but if I was, I can assure you that it was all unnecessary. There was never the slightest possibility of me listening. I remember what it was like back in 1955, when Grace Archer was killed in the programme. I was not in that particular episode because I was doing another recording at the time with Pauline Seville, the actress who plays Mrs P in The Archers, and when we heard the programme that night, we both wept buckets. I really felt heartbroken and could not believe that it had happened. Obviously I could not have coped with listening to Doris—myself—dying. I felt very, very sad that she had to die. More than that, I felt very, very bitter. I hated the thought of dying and I hated everyone whom I thought responsible for killing me off. At the time, I am quite sure I could not distinguish between Gwen and Doris. It must have been some kind of madness because I remember hating 'him'—some man who was my

4

murderer, but I did not even know who I meant by 'him' and in fact, I still do not know.

Before that awful 'death', the thing that had most worried me about leaving The Archers was the prospect of losing touch with all my colleagues. I could not bear the thought of not seeing them all and not being part of everything. You see, over the years I have had several long spells of illness when I could not get to the studios for recording sessions, and that always left me very miserable. I used to get really frustrated and very bad-tempered so I knew that if I was like that because of temporary breaks, I was going to have a really bad time if I gave up permanently. I know I had been talking about retiring for several years. In fact, I see from a cutting from my local newspaper in January, 1976, that I had decided to stop on my seventieth birthday later that year. I suppose that might have been the sensible thing to do but, of course, I didn't! Instead I carried on making the long journey from Torquay to Birmingham, although it got more and more uncomfortable because of my arthritis. Still, I was, I thought, being the real professional, always making sure that the show went on. And, in all honesty, I think I did go on giving something to the programme and its millions of listeners.

The consequence of all my bravery or foolhardiness, whichever it was, came one day in February 1980. I arrived at the studio not feeling very bright and I remember that I was not at my best on the recording. During the interval between episodes, I was talking to the producer and apologizing for several stumbles I had made in delivering the dialogue when he said, in a jokey kind of way, words to the effect, 'Don't worry, Gwen, if you don't want to carry on, we can always do that death scene.' I know he was not being serious and I know that I had often said that I would quite like to play Doris's death when the time came, but on that particular day I suddenly felt ever so frightened. I think I might have felt too close to the end of everything to see the funny side. I had not felt well to start with, but by then I was quite ill. I do not quite know how I got myself on to the train for the homeward journey, but I remember not being able to read the station sign when I eventually arrived in Torquay.

After that everything is just a jumble of doctors and nurses and hospital smells and lots of faces, until I found myself in the nursing home suffering the after-effects of a stroke. It was a terrible shock and I just cried and cried and cried. I know now that I had yet another stroke afterwards, which made matters even worse. I lost the use of one of my arms and my leg was paralysed too, but the most shattering blow of all—especially to a radio actress—was the damage to my speech. I could not talk in complete sentences any more. I knew what I wanted to say all right, but the words would not come out in the right order. Everyone was terribly kind, especially my brother, Trevor, who came in to see me every single day, but really nothing could ease the awful, awful frustration.

Whoever said: 'Hope springs eternal,' is wrong. At that moment I knew there was no hope of me ever working again as an actress, nor was there much likelihood of me leading anything like my former life. I cannot begin to describe the terrible despair and anger that engulfed me. Certainly I felt, instead, that I ought to have died. I could see no justice in being allowed to live when my life had been destroyed. It was all too cruel for me. Under the circumstances, is it any wonder that I did not contemplate, even for a moment, the possibility of listening to the fateful programme in which the other—and until then, intact—half of me just slipped quietly into eternity? I had had enough real misery without soaking up any more agony from a daily soap opera on the radio, although at the time I did not see it as simply as that. The two things, my illness and Doris's death, were fused together in my mind and I am sure it was a completely automatic safety valve that stopped me listening rather than any rational decision.

I have got back into the habit of listening to

the programme again most evenings. It is still very good and I love it. But I am still very sad that Doris is not there either. The Archers is very important to many of its listeners, more so than you would expect for a radio programme, I think it offers a kind of comfortable security when society seems to be going through so many changes. For those people, Doris Archer seemed to have a special appeal, representing as she did a sort of idealized motherhood. Everyone could admire and love her despite—or maybe because of—her funny, old-fashioned ways, and she was also a link with the past when family-ties and morals seemed so much stronger. I think her absence upsets the balance of things a bit and I have noticed a tendency for the story to drift away from the Archer family on to some of the other villagers and from the older characters to the younger ones. I know things cannot go on the same way forever, but the listeners always did love the Archer family more than most of the others and I think it is a pity to change the emphasis too much.

The public reaction to my own illness and the subsequent death of Doris Archer really amazed me, and I think it played an important part in seeing me through the darkest days. I had been used to a fair amount of attention from the listeners and the press. In fact in the fifties and early sixties, before television really got hold, I was something of a star and I have a collection of photographs, press clippings and fan letters to prove it. But all that left me totally unprepared for what happened when news of my illness and its implications for the programme leaked out. Because of the recording schedules, the last episode I did, on that awful day in February, 1980, was not heard on the air until April, and for some time after the the scriptwriters kept me around Ambridge but never quite on centre stage, so that few people noticed my absence. By September I was being missed and listeners started to ask questions so that the BBC had to say that I was ill. That led to a tiny paragraph in one national newspaper and quite a lot of letters, cards and get-well messages. Then Richard Last wrote a piece for the front page of the *Daily Telegraph* which hinted for the first time at the implications for the programme—that Doris Archer might never appear again. The balloon went up. It seemed every newspaper in the country wanted constant information about my state of health and journalists started hanging around the nursing home. I was cocooned from all this, partly by the staff and partly by my illness, which left me quite confused half of the time. But I was not cut off from the public's response—letters and cards by every post and enough flowers to keep a florist in business for weeks. And, of course, it made me cry. Well, there I had been for months wallowing in self-pity, feeling trapped in my small bedroom.

9

Everyone, it seemed, had forgotten me. My only visitors were my brother and his family and one or two close friends. I did not know, of course, that everyone else was being warned off because of my condition. In my sorry state, my loneliness was just evidence that nobody cared about me any more. When the letters started to come, it was really wonderful and when wonderful things happen to an actress, tears are inevitable.

Although it was not intentional, we—the BBC and myself—led the press a merry dance during that September and October. When I finally decided to retire from the programme, I told my brother and then asked one of the nurses to write to the BBC for me. My brother simply accepted my decision as the only sensible thing to do, but the BBC suggested that I thought it over for a while because they thought I was only trying to let them off the hook. So when the press started inquiring, the BBC said: 'No, Miss Berryman has not left The Archers,' and down in Torquay, the opposite answer was being given. The stories and the headlines built up even more extensively than in 1955, when the programme was in its heyday and Grace Archer's death was front-page news. I only learned all this later, when the BBC gave me an enormous scrapbook with a selection of the thousands of newspaper cuttings.

Somewhere along the line, the BBC did

accept that I would not be coming back and made arrangements to write Doris out of the script. In their usual way, they would have done that in some secrecy and I can just see them going through all the business of producing only a limited number of scripts, carefully logging who they were issued to and then demanding their return as soon as the recording session was finished. We always did it that way when there was something special in the programme that we did not want to give away to the listeners. In the past the security always worked and on this occasion it nearly did, breaking down only at the very last moment and not, I believe, because of anyone close to the programme. On the Saturday before the 'death' episode was due to be broadcast on the Monday, it was again the *Daily Telgraph* that revealed what was to happen: Doris Archer would die peacefully in her armchair while Dan was at church, and she would be found by granddaughter Shula. The paper also revealed that a special funeral service had been recorded in a little Warwickshire church, with the local congregation standing in for the villagers of Ambridge.

The rest of the press went wild, there were headlines and pictures in all the national and most of the provincial papers. The story also made the main news on BBC television and radio and it even attracted leaders in several of the big papers. The *Sunday Times*, for example, said:

Gwen Berryman, the actress who has played the role of the matriarch of the Archer family ever since that radio soap opera began, nearly thirty years ago, is unwell and not likely to return to the broadcasting studio. Since it is unthinkable that anyone else can be Doris Archer, her part is to be written out of the script.

The Archers are special, no doubt about that. Not since Conan Doyle put Sherlock Holmes, Dr Watson and Mrs Hudson into 221B Baker Street have fictional characters and places commanded such widespread suspension of unbelief. People identify with the characters and write letters to them as though, like Holmes, they were real flesh and blood. *Aficionados*—three million of them—pounce like lynxes on any deviation from the sacred norm.

Considering the un-feverish pace at which Ambridge life proceeds and the size of the ripples induced upon its tranquil surface by even the smallest incident, there seems no reason why the Archers should not continue indefinitely. But here is a difficulty. Even fictional characters age. Doris Archer was 'born' in 1900, her husband Dan in 1896. Grandparents and great-grandparents, they cannot remain forever, frozen like fossils in a glacier. Though we wish Miss Berryman a return to health and years of content, Doris

Archer herself has reached the end of the road. Her passing will be comparable with Trollope's killing off of Mrs Proudie, and much more regrettable.

That was under the headline: 'Alas, Poor Doris', and the *News of the World* said simply: 'Bye, Doris', and then added:

Doris Archer is to die from a heart attack at the age of eighty tomorrow. All good wishes go to Gwen Berryman, who has played the part for thirty years. She quits because of illness. May she soon recover to enjoy her retirement and her memories of a wonderful radio programme.

Just when it looked as if the clamour would subside, there came another twist that excited the newspapers. The actors' union, Equity, complained about the use of the church congregation singing in the funeral service on the programme.

The *Daily Express* made the row the main story on the front page and under the banner headline: 'BBC's Black Farce', they reported:

Just when everyone was ready for a good cry over the drama of Doris Archer's death on radio last night, a union turned it into black farce. You can't have that village church congregation singing the final hymn, said Equity: You must use our members. Day-long crisis followed at the BBC's Birmingham studios. In the end three million listeners tuned into the The Archers, heard the tear-jerking end without realizing the script had been changed at the last minute. But the actors' union is also threatening Thursday's episode on Doris's funeral. Fact has a habit of being stranger than fiction in this 'Everyday story of country folk'. The death episode was recorded a month ago because of the need to 'write out' seventy-four-year-old actress Gwen Berryman, the actress who has played Doris for thirty years and is now too ill to carry on.

Last night, Gwen was in Torquay—watching *Angels* on TV—as Doris died peacefully in her favourite armchair in Glebe Cottage, Ambridge. Dan Archer had gone to evensong, and the final scene was of his daughter Chris and granddaughter Shula going to the church to break the news. As a background, the BBC had recorded the congregation of the thirteenth-century Church of St John the Baptist in the Warwickshire village of Cherington singing Hymn 33, A & M, 'The day thou gavest, Lord, is ended . . .' And that meant trouble.

In London, Equity's organizer, Mr Glen Barnham, said: 'The recordings made by the villagers of Cherington have been blacked.' Professional singers, union members should have been used. At first stunned BBC chiefs thought that, despite all the advance publicity, they would have to postpone the episode. Then they decided to make a new recording.

And for good measure, the *Express* printed an editorial on which they had the headline: 'Sour Face of Equity'.

For the three million regular listeners of The Archers, the death of Doris Archer was a serious affair. As it was for the countless others who have listened to the series at some point in their lives. It was left to Equity, the actors' trade union, to turn it into a farce. Because the BBC had recorded a congregation in a genuine country church singing a hymn, Equity threatened to 'black' the programme. They were not Equity members, you see. Well, we have all heard of restrictive practices, but this is ridiculous. Does Equity really believe that the use of ordinary people on occasion is a threat to their livelihood and their professional pride? In the event, the BBC had a day of panic-stricken efforts to sort it out—ending up by using a recording made twenty years ago. Let Doris Archer rest in peace, not in restrictive practices.

Even *The Times*, usually quite restrained in these matters, launched forth, albeit tongue-in-cheek:

So Doris Archer dies and pat comes Equity to mar the funeral. At Pebble Mill, the BBC's

Birmingham factory to which Ambridge looks for its predestined life, they publicly deplore the intrusion: a shame not to let the old lady die in peace. But Equity, which knows a publicity stunt when it sees one, wants a slice of the action. Its members have had two thousand fewer engagements in radio drama this year than last, according to Mr Peter Plouviez, its general secretary. Are they to be expected to stand idly by while the scabs who attend morning service at the church of St John the Baptist, Cherington, Warwickshire, supply the funeral rendering of 'The day thou gavest, Lord, is ended', always Doris's favourite? Better a gramophone record, on which the Performing Rights Society collects. Better still, the inappropriately cultivated voices of the professional BBC singers. But they were busy recording something else in St Giles's, Cripplegate, in the City of London, unaccompanied as it happened; and no organist could be found. So back to the studio.

Life, as it can be depended upon to do, has again trumped art. The imaginary mourning of Ambridge has had to make way for Equity's unimaginable talent for farce. All along, one has heard, many of the programme's regulars have experienced difficulty in distinguishing the real from the radio world. If Dan Archer needed a new cowman or Doris a daily, the applications flooded in—not for the part, for the job. What are they to make of the latest chapter of events? The village of Ambridge obviously possesses a solid reality which no one would be inclined to attribute to Pebble Mill—though it might just be a property at the other end of the country which city folk have bought and are doing up for weekends. And who is this fellow Plouviez with his made-up name? Some bounder from London who has moved in and means to do old Walter Whatsisname out of his second pair of corduroys, most likely. The Vicar has had to have a word with him already.

It is only fair to say that Mr Plouviez was quick to respond, with a sting in the tail of his letter which maintained the element of wit that many thought lacking in earlier comments from Equity:

Sir, Because my newspapers are not delivered, I first heard of your editorial 'A Death in Ambridge' (29 October) on a BBC early-morning news programme. The short quotation they gave indicated that you were making a serious, if not actually vicious, attack on Equity. I quickly drafted a reply, dripping with outrage and containing an odd snide passage or two of comment on the peculiarly inopportune moment *The Times* had chosen to give advice on industrial relations.

When eventually I read the whole piece, I was

delighted to see with what elegant wit you had debunked and deflated the whole nonsensical and I believe BBC-inspired stunt.

However, I deeply resent the allegation that my name is 'made up'. How such a suggestion can be made by a newspaper whose editor we are expected to believe is called Rees-Mogg is beyond me, but rest assured that you will hear more of this matter when, as we trade unionists are wont to say, my executive has met. Yours faithfully, Peter Plouviez, General Secretary, British Actors' Equity Association.

The *Daily Telegraph*, which, as I mentioned earlier, started all the newspaper coverage, thought they would try to restore some sanity to their pages at least. They headed their editorial: 'Nil Nisi Bunkum'.

We do not express our deep regret at the death of Doris Archer. We refrain from doing so for the reason that she cannot have died since she was never alive. This brutal concession to the literal truth may seem to some to be insensitive and even heartless; but after the fuss of the last few days, the hazardous duty of placing it on record is surely one which no newspaper, with even a residual concern for the nation's sanity, can properly escape.

Tragedy, we know, can purge and exalt the soul, and there is no shame in the feelings aroused in civilized human beings by the suicide of Anna Karenina or the madness of Ophelia. But this kind of disciplined indulgence of the imagination is a different matter from the prolonged excursion into self-induced fantasy in which many people would seem to have been engaging since the *Daily Telegraph* mercilessly announced Mrs Archer's forthcoming death. Indeed, the only clear note of sanity which seems to have been struck on this subject was supplied by the actors' union, Equity. They complained of the use of an ordinary Sunday church congregation to sing hymns at Doris's funeral. In fact, they took the almost incredibly matter-of-fact view that the funeral was part of a broadcast play for which only fully-unionized actors should be employed. This earned them the dignified reproach of a BBC official: 'It is very regrettable and a great pity that Doris is not allowed to die in peace.'

So much for Doris slipping away quietly! Luckily I wasn't really aware all the fuss was going on, but I did reap the benefits of all the lovely letters and cards and flowers. My only sadness on that score was that because of my paralysed arm and hand, I was never able to write back to them all personally. I know I will never be able to repay all the kindnesses I have received and I hope that all my friends across the land will see this book as something of an acknowledgement for their generosity of thought and deed at a time when I needed them so badly.

But all this sounds very much like the end of the story, and while that may be the case, it is a story that also has a beginning and a middle.

CHAPTER TWO

The stories of both Gwen Berryman and Doris Archer go back a long way before that New Year's Day in 1951 when the BBC Light Programme launched its new daily serial, The Archers, making me something of a star and her the wireless audience's favourite mother. Although we were disparate souls—she the very essence of the country wife, me the out-and-out townie who remained unmarried—there have been many parallels in our backgrounds that are not always the contrivance of scriptwriters.

To set the scene for my own story, I want to go back exactly a hundred years, to when my father was born, because he was undoubtedly the greatest influence in my life and it was what happened during his own childhood that made that influence so potent.

Richard Edward Berryman was born in 1881 in the 'Black Country' of Staffordshire. He was the youngest of five children and his father kept a greengrocer's shop which gave the family a very moderate living. I do not know a lot about his mother, but it would appear from information I have managed to gather that she was a beautiful woman, very much the spirit of the house. She died when Richard was about five and her husband promptly began to go to pieces. He took to the bottle. In those far-away days, if a man took to the bottle, he usually did it in a big way. Grandfather was no exception. He drank himself silly. Perhaps the first clear picture of the family is one of hungry children sitting on the doorstep waiting for the man who was trying, and failing hopelessly, to forget his worries.

This precarious mode of living could not last. The neighbours (filled with the then-fashionable sense of 'clinging together' against the common threat of poverty) who brought food to the kids merely postponed the inevitable. The family was eventually split up. Two of the children were adopted by relatives, two by strangers and little Richard was put into an institution known as the Cottage Home, in Wolverhampton. He was seven when this happened and his only memories of happiness were of the occasional picnic on Penn Common in the days when his mother was alive and everything seemed beautiful and eternal. The rest of his memories were grim and depressing but, in the end, it may have been those experiences that built character.

It was in the Cottage Home that a happening took place which, although apparently so normal, was of the greatest significance. *Father heard a man blow a trumpet.* There never was a braver, more lasting blast. The boy decided there and then that one day he too would have a trumpet. I cannot tell you exactly the sort of life he lived in the home, but there was the fashionable discipline of those Victorian days, the hardness, the communal existence. There was, though, a more pleasing side; the odd coppers which he received for fetching the matron her drop of gin. Sometimes he received a penny for this secret service. Sometimes, if the matron had imbibed before he went to replenish the stock, she was known to have given him threepence. The money was promptly placed in the Trumpet Fund. Another plus was that the home gave my father the means of earning his living. He was put to work with the resident shoe-repairer, the very man who had the trumpet. It was not the sound of this man's horn that woke Dad from his bed—they had a much more efficient, though less-romantic way—but he did have more opportunities to hear the trumpet and his determination to buy one for himself was strengthened.

Dad was still just a boy when he left the home to start work. He became apprenticed to a certain Mr George Smith, shoe-maker and repairer, at an agreed wage of sixpence per week and all found. His working days were long. The number of hours was not specified in the apprenticeship indentures. His day started at six am and ended when the boss gave permission to stop. This was not because Mr Smith was a particularly hard man. He was simply a product of his time. He employed several other men, ran a fair business and was a decent citizen. He accepted the responsibility of bringing my father up in a righteous way, and with this in mind, saw to it that twopence of his weekly wage was put into the church collecting-plate every Sunday. The handling of the other fourpence he left to the lad himself. Dad saved twopence and used the other twopence to buy eggs because the Smiths never had eggs on the menu!

Dad was a careful man, but on one occasion he did break out. His savings had reached seven shillings and sixpence when a fair came to Wolverhampton. A fair meant a great deal more in those days than it does now and Dad visited this dazzling display of money-traps and parted company with his seven and six in less than twenty minutes. For days afterwards, he walked about stunned with remorse, asking himself why he had done such a foolish thing and being unable to answer. 'Never,' he told himself, 'never will I spend all my money again.' He was young, his longing for a trumpet had not waned and with characteristic patience and determination, he started to save his odd coppers again. No matter what sort of fair came afterwards, no matter how seductive the attractions, he was never again influenced.

At this stage, I must tell you about Mr Smith's son, Georgie, because he was to be important in the life of my father. He played the violin and at a very tender age was considered to be something of an infant prodigy. There seems no doubt that his command of his instrument was something very out of the ordinary and it was perhaps only the incident of a physical deformity that prevented him from reaching the heights. I introduce him to you because of the help he gave my father in an awkward situation that could have had an effect on me in later years.

The money Dad was able to put into the trumpet fund increased; he was getting older and he received more from his master. In addition he decreased the waiting by doing without most of the things they say make life worth living these days. At long last the moment arrived. There was enough in the fund to buy the trumpet. Dad dashed off to the music shop where the proprietor, who knew all about it, had the glittering trumpet ready. It was a great moment when he arrived back at Mr Smith's with his prize, the rewards of a lifetime of saving. At the very first opportunity he tried it out. Horrible noises filled the place, but Dad was not worried. He knew that he would put this right with practice. But if Dad did not mind, Mr Smith did. 'Get that thing out of this house,' he yelled. Dad did not plead or show frustration. The instrument was put back into its case and a forlorn little fellow went back to the music shop. He returned with a flute. Mr Smith cared less for the wood than he did for the brass. He repeated his previous order and back went the flute. It was at this moment that the violinist son, Georgie, suggested to his father that young Berryman might be allowed to have a cello and that he would do the teaching. A conference of all interested parties was called and the proposition thoroughly discussed. The outcome was that a room, at a rent of one shilling and sixpence per week, was to be placed at the disposal of my father so that he could practise in his spare time. The way Dad set to work to master the instrument is one of the best things he ever did. The midnight oil was burned with a vengeance and before long the initial shrieks became notes, the notes blended into melody and there was music for violin and cello to be heard most evenings in the Smiths' house. The man in the music shop was delighted at the progress Dad made and one day he offered him a booking—playing in a dance orchestra at the local town hall. For this engagement my father received the significant sum of seven shillings and sixpence. At long last, he felt the sin of wasting a similar amount at the fair had been expunged.

Rockefeller could never have had the kick from his fortune that Dad had from this sum. He was, he felt, in the big-money class. By the time all this came to pass, of course, he was a young man, out of his apprenticeship, with more skill at boot-making than Dr Manette, and with a careful eye on a system of payment known these days as an incentive bonus. 'Make more shoes,' said Mr Smith in effect, 'and I shall give you more money.' However, it was the extra money he made from his musical engagements that made it possible for him to take his next step. He had saved seventy pounds (plus eighteen shillings and sixpence which he left with Mr Smith, just in case it was ever needed) when he fell in love, as quickly and determinedly as he had once made up his mind to have a trumpet. He saw a girl with gorgeous red hair. Something happened inside himself more lovely than any of the notes he could produce on his cello. He followed her home (a highly irregular procedure), he spoke to her before he had been introduced (again highly irregular), and she, probably alarmed by such flouting of convention, threatened him with her big strong brothers. At that, he beat a strategic retreat.

But it was spring in Wolverhampton and thereafter Dad laid siege to the wonderful redhead named Louise. She lived on a small-holding surrounded by a high wall. Dad used to climb on this wall and patiently gaze at the distant house, hoping that *she* would see him there and come out. Sometimes she did, and sometimes she sent one of the big strong brothers to make a show. But I am sure that they were all quite fond of the little fellow on the wall, who faded like a shadow at their approach but appeared again the next day as surely as the seasons. The persistence which could wait a lifetime for a trumpet and be satisfied with a cello could take an affair of this sort in its stride. In those days of advance and retreat, he told the redhead what he felt and she must have believed him, because she consented to become his girl.

Then one day he saw a business offered for sale in the shoe-making line at a very reasonable price of sixty pounds. The following night he bought it. It was with very mixed feelings that he broke the news to Mr Smith that their long industrial association was over. After all, Mr Smith's house had been his home. The focal point of his planning, struggling and successes. He was not prepared for the reaction. The shoe-maker boiled over with temper. He walked about shouting: 'All these years I have nourished a viper in my bosom!' Then he seized all my father's things and threw them into the street, some through the upstairs window and others through the door. He ranted and raved:

'Get out and never let me see your face again.'
He was to see my father again, when Dad twice
rescued him from bankruptcy. But that is
another story.

Dad was able to rent a small house and then
he asked the redhead to share it with him, as his
wife. 'I come without a penny,' he told her. She
looked at his disreputable collar. 'I think I had
better marry you,' she said, 'so that I can look
after you.'

The redhead was, of course, my mother. She
was not altogether in favour of Dad buying the
business. She issued a gentle warning to which
he listened and paid no attention. For the rest of
her life with him, she issued similar warnings
whenever he had these urges to do something
and he took no more notice of her then than he
did the first time. In his business ventures, he
was always right just as she was always wrong.

When I arrived on the scene—on 23
November, 1906, the day of St Cecilia, patron
saint of music—they had been married for two
years and were quite well set up in a little shop
in Salop Street, Wolverhampton. They lived in
what we would now call a flat above the shop,
and above that was an attic workshop where
Dad had twelve repairers hammering away most
of the day. Somewhere in the midst of all this
there were two pianos, which Dad played when
he was not practising on the cello.

How much the musical background

influenced me becomes obvious from my very earliest childhood recollection. My mother was an expert needlewoman and used to make my bonnets, and I remember going in to the shop next door to ours to show off to the lady there. That shop sold gramophones and bicycles, an odd combination made even odder by the slogan on the counter: 'No orange boxes.' The owner was a man called Len Walker, and whenever I went in, his wife would lift me up on to her kitchen table to admire my bonnet. If the gramophone in the shop was going, I used to dance and whirl around on the table top. I don't quite know why I did that because no one ever showed me how to dance. I think it was just instinct.

A couple of years later, when I was five and the youngest pupil at the local primary school, I had another experience that seemed to point me relentlessly towards a career as a performer of some kind. It was just before Christmas when, after weeks of careful preparation, the school presented its annual concert. On the night, everyone backstage was running around in a state of high nervous tension—except for me. I did not have the faintest idea what all the bother and fuss was about as I sat there contentedly nursing my new golliwog. I had been given the golliwog specially for the concert and I was also wearing a brand new nightdress and had my hair tied up in curl-rags. I was not the slightest bit nervous and when I was told it was my turn, I took my golliwog and a candlestick made to look as if it were alight, went in front of the curtains and sang 'Goodnight, Golly'. When I was finished, I just turned to leave the stage because I knew nothing about applause or audience reaction. I thought I was just doing what I had been doing for a long time at home and could not really understand what all the noise was. One of the teachers stopped me from retreating, made me take a bow and presented me with a lovely box of chocolates, which, I remember to this day, was tied with pink and dark-brown ribbon and had a spray of almond blossoms on the lid. At that, I evidently abandoned the golliwog and the candlestick right in the middle of the stage, much to everyone's amusement. My father said later that I then told him that if ladies who sang on stage were always given such lovely presents, that was what I wanted to do when I grew up. If true, it was quite a prophetic comment. In fact, this was the first stirrings of my ambition to become an opera singer.

Another memory of those days also gains significance only in retrospect. I went to Wolverhampton Girls' High School when I was seven and every day I used to walk the mile or so from home to school with three or four other girls. One of the girls was called Edith, and she had a flair for telling stories. They were so good that she kept us enthralled for the whole journey, which took us about quarter of an hour. When she found longer stories, it meant we walked to school more slowly and were often in danger of being late—until she had the brainwave of breaking them up into episodes and telling us a bit each day. It was my first introduction to a daily serial. I do not know if Edith ever became a writer, but I am sure she would have qualified for The Archers.

There was not even a BBC then—it did not start until a couple of years later, in 1922—so far from any thoughts of radio work, I continued determinedly towards a career as a singer, although I did also learn to play the cello, to keep my father happy. I left school at seventeen, with quite a fair academic career behind me and clutching a hard-earned School Certificate.

I spent two very happy years at the Birmingham School of Music but then, not long after my twenty-first birthday party, I made the journey to London to take up the place I had been offered at the Royal Academy of Music. I could not have been more excited as I left Wolverhampton with a large trunk, a collection of bags, my cello and a guarantee of a weekly allowance of three pounds from my father.

I did enjoy my days as a student in London. It was the first time—apart from the odd holiday—that I had ever been away from home and once I got used to not having my mother to look after me and my young brother to fuss

31

over, I enjoyed the freedom to be able to come and go as I pleased.

I shared a room with a girl called Ethel Evans from Pontypridd. She and several other girls in the house were also at the Academy and we all became very close friends. Friendship was very important in those days because although most of us received money from home, we really did suffer a fair amount of hardship. I remember my first winter there. It was so cold, the water jugs in the bedrooms froze solid and we had to huddle together for warmth. Quite often we did not have enough money for food and I used to be an expert in dividing two-egg omelettes into six helpings.

But poverty never stopped us from indulging in our favourite pastime—going to the opera at Sadler's Wells or to the Old Vic theatre. We used to get seats in 'the gods' for sevenpence and every now and again we even had enough to buy one lollipop between us. I wonder what the other patrons thought as the sticky thing was passed backwards and forwards along the row.

When we were not having that kind of high life, we practised and practised and practised. There was a piano in the front room at the digs and we used to have to take turns at using it. In the end, we got very frustrated and decided we ought to have a second piano. The landlady, not unnaturally, said she would not buy it but, being a smashing lady, agreed to set another room aside if we cared to buy one ourselves. Having being the joint-buyers of penny-lollipops and other communal necessities, we were experts in pooling resources, but when it came to the piano, we had to acknowledge our shortcomings. Then one of the girls had a brainwave—why not hire one? We all headed for Selfridges, but when we got to the piano department and were confronted by the stiff-necked assistant and even stiffer hire charges, we ran out of courage and fled empty-handed. Back at the digs we had another meeting and finally decided that just one of us would go to Selfridges and pretend to be very well off and ask to have a piano on approval with a view to buying it. I lost the argument and next day found myself being pushed in through the main entrance to the store. Screwing up my courage, I put on what I thought was a very French accent and haughtily told the sycophantic assistant that I rather liked one of the upright pianos but I could not be sure if it was exactly right until I saw and heard it in my own home. It worked like a treat: the assistant insisted that I must have it delivered on approval, 'If mademoiselle will just give her name and address?' I had not thought that far and my broken French all but disintegrated. Luckily the saleswoman was obviously too interested in the commission from the prospective sale to notice the Englishness of my name and the seediness of my north London address. The piano was duly delivered and we got several weeks of extra practice before the company gave up the idea of making a sale and came and took it away again.

All the practice must have done me a lot of good and I did well at the Academy. I gained first the Bronze and then the Silver medals in the performer (singer) category, then I got the Certificate of Merit (the Academy's highest award), and went on to win, despite very stiff competition, the Westmoreland Scholarship, the Isabel Jay Gold Medal and the Acton-Bond prize.

During that period, I also had my first professional engagement—singing in the chorus of *Samson and Delilah* at Bournemouth Winter Gardens—and I fell in love!

I cannot remember how much I earned for my Bournemouth performance. It certainly would not have been very much, but it did not matter in the slightest, because it allowed me one more step up the ladder. My ambition to become an opera singer was closer to realization.

Falling in love I do remember all about. It was a wonderful experience, which I am quite sure had much more romance to it than you might expect today. I met the young man when he came to lodge in the house in north London. Although he had the very Scottish christian name of Munro, he was very, very Welsh. He had been raised in the singing valleys and music

34

was as much part of his life as it was mine. But it was another element of Welsh culture that first brought us together—rugby. He was a keen player—with the London Welsh second XV—and the first time he brought his mud-caked strip home to wash, he stopped-up the waste-pipe! I was delegated by the angry household to remonstrate with him and to ensure that it did not happen again. It did not—he was so good-looking and so charmingly apologetic that I ended up offering to do his washing for him! It did not take me long to fall head-over-heels in love and when I learned that he had excellent career prospects—he was training to be a doctor—it all seemed perfect. I knew he was the very sort of man my father would have wanted me to marry.

It was quite idyllic. We saw each other every day—always chaperoned by our friends because this was still the 1920s—and I went to see him play rugby and he came to hear me sing in the various concerts and recitals.

Love was obviously good for my voice, because I picked up several good notices from the prestigious magazine *Musical Opinion*: 'Further interest was centred on a young Wolverhampton soprano, Gwen Berryman (a student of the RAM) who sang superbly. She possessed an excellent and well trained voice, which is admirably controlled and manipulated, and if this performance is any criterion of her capabilities, she promises to go far.' That was for a performance in Mendelssohn's *St Paul*, and after another concert the paper's critic said, 'Vocal solos were contributed by Miss Gwen Berryman, whose singing of "Solvieg's Song" (Grieg) and "Batti-batti" (from Mozart's *Don Giovanni*) was well nigh impeccable.'

It was all very encouraging and I have to confess that I loved all the compliments and seeing my name in the paper. It more than made up for my physical shortcomings—well I wasn't exactly sylph-like! In fact, sometimes my friends were a bit insensitive in the way they referred to my figure, which I always thought of as *ample* but always described as *plumpish*. One day a crowd of the girls were going to an audition and they tried to persuade me to join them. 'Come along, Gwen. There may be a part for a fat girl,' said one of them. The jibe was unintentional, so I did go along, but just for the ride, really. Of course I did not get the part I tried for—that of a chorus girl. Whoever heard of ample chorus girls? However, the producer did seem impressed by my singing. I always remember his disembodied voice booming up from the darkened stalls of the theatre: 'I like your voice,' but then he added what I thought was a very unfair rider: 'I don't like the song. Get another!' It was unfair because I did not have any other music with me and therefore could not sing another song. All I could do was laugh and joke my way out of it, but I left the theatre feeling a bit low and an awful lot less sure of myself than I had been when I first took to the stage.

At home the next day, however, I discovered one of the special ingredients that was to keep me in that funny thing called show business for the rest of my life. I call it the fairy-tale twist. Answering a knock on the door, I found a telegram boy with a telegram for me—it was the first I had ever received and I was terrified. Telegrams meant good news or bad news and as I was not expecting any good news, this, I was convinced, must be bad. Instead, it was the producer's theatrical way of inviting me back for another audition, this time for an acting part.

He had been impressed by my sense of fun—one of God's compensations to the heavyweights—and asked me to read the leading part. The show was A. P. Herbert's *Derby Day* and Mrs Bones, the female lead, is a Cockney. I just could not get the accent right—remember I was not an actress and my natural accent was rooted very firmly in the Midlands. I think the producer was as disappointed as I, because he offered me a smaller part and said that if I worked on the Cockney voice, I could understudy Mabel Constandurous. She was one of the great names of the theatre and I was absolutely thrilled. My acting debut was in that show at the Lyric Theatre, Hammersmith, and although in the rudest of health, Mabel Constandurous feigned 'indisposition' to let me take the centre stage on just one night—and she sent me a bouquet as well.

My cup really would have overflowed if my mother could have shared my father's enthusiasm. She did not. She desperately wanted me to make my career on the concert platform and implored me not to go on the stage. Although I found it very difficult to ignore her advice, it turned out to be the most important decision I ever made.

For a couple of years, I continued training at the Academy and taking operatic lessons from an Italian teacher—they cost thirty shillings each and that seemed like a king's ransom to me. I supplemented my father's allowance by taking whatever singing and acting parts I could get. I even made my debut in films, in *Looking on the Bright Side*, starring Gracie Fields. That was great fun, although it was only a tiny part, singing in the chorus. I enjoyed all the hustle and bustle of the film set and discovered how dreams were packaged in front of cardboard scenery that looked dangerously shaky every time my comfortable figure brushed it. My disappointment came when I saw the film. Oh, I was still in it all right; I had not ended up on the cutting-room floor. But what I had not realized was that in putting focus on the star, the camera only saw me and the rest of the gang as a blur of faces.

As my career progressed, so did my romance with my wonderful Welshman. His gaiety and zest for living were infectious and almost all the time we spent together, we seemed to be singing or laughing. After the shaky start he had become very popular with everyone else in the house and he was very protective towards all the girls, whom he treated like sisters. When one of them had trouble with an abscess under a tooth, it was Munro who actually saved her life. Yvette, who was from the south of France, went to a dentist when the abscess developed but he did not treat it properly and her face swelled up like a melon. She was obviously in some pain and I asked Munro for advice. He took one look at her and called for an ambulance and had her rushed to hospital. The doctors there said they were only just in time to save her life. As it was, she was so seriously ill that she spent almost four months in hospital. When she got out, Munro helped her with a claim for compensation from the dentist. She won the case and was awarded £275. Yvette was so grateful for all Munro had done that she invited both of us to spend a long summer holiday at her parents' home in Cannes. It was the first foreign trip for both of us and we had a lovely time. It gave me a taste for travel which stayed with me throughout my life.

My parents had also fallen victim to Munro's charm and when he finally qualified as a doctor and asked me to marry him, they were as delighted as I was ecstatic. We became engaged and fixed the wedding date for the following year. I was blissfully happy and I felt that I now knew just how my father had reacted all those years ago when he first saw his beautiful redhead. For me, too, it seemed that spring had come to stay.

Sadly, my spring was to be almost as brief as the actual season, and it was followed not by any summer warmth but by the most bitter winter imaginable. Munro became seriously ill and died.

After qualifying, he had gone to work as a junior doctor in a children's fever hospital and somewhere along the way picked up some kind of chest infection. It was first diagnosed as pneumonia, then pleurisy and finally tuberculosis. He became gradually weaker and weaker and it broke my heart to watch his energies fade away. It seemed doubly tragic that someone who went to such pains to keep fit— regular training sessions and rugby every week—should become so frail. But, as I nursed him, I never once thought he was going to die. It never entered my head: I was distressed enough seeing him looking so poorly.

Although I knew *he* was never going to get back to normal—in those days there was little they could do about TB, except send people to a sanatorium—I tried hard to maintain some kind of normality in my own career and after one audition I was offered a big part playing opposite George Robey in a show called *The Jolly Roger*. I was delighted and rushed to the hospital, where Munro was being treated, to give him the good news. I knew he would be very pleased for me. But when I got there, I was told he was too ill for visitors. He died the next day.

From the heavy heights of professional success, I plunged to the very depths of personal despair. There are really no words to describe how I felt, and even now all the clichés would still be inadequate. My bright, shiny little world disintegrated. I became very ill when my emotional collapse was compounded by pneumonia. I did the only possible thing: I fled London, my career and my happy memories. I crawled deep into my family back in Wolverhampton.

Time did what nothing and no one else could. It smoothed away some of the roughest edges of the nightmare. My parents had moved to a bigger house and the large garden was a godsend, because I could sit out there and quietly unscramble my demented thoughts. After something like six months my grief was still unabated, but I had learned to accept the situation and to realize that life was going to go on whatever I did. Inevitably, it was my father who put me back on an even keel. Over the years, as his business acumen increased he had acquired several properties around the town and one of these was a vacant shop next door to his own shoe-repairing business. He gave me eighty pounds, the tenancy of the shop, lots of advice and prodded me into the hard world of commerce, as proprietress of a little drapery store. It was just what I needed. I knew very little about selling and I had to work very hard to get things going. Concentrating on how to buy and control stock, on how to price items profitably and on how to keep the books all took my mind off other things. I followed my father's advertising campaign, printing my own leaflets and then going around the houses at night stuffing them through letterboxes. It was very therapeutic and moderately successful.

My confidence was given another boost when, a few months later, I was offered a small part in a play at the local Grand Theatre put on by the visiting Salberg repertory company from Birmingham. The visit to Wolverhampton was something of an experiment and I suspect the offer to me was engineered by a friend. I also suspect it was made out of sympathy rather than from any real expectation of a great performance. In fact Leon Salberg, who ran the company, did not know I had been a professional actress. He thought I was a talented amateur and at the end of the first week, when the others were given their modest pay envelopes, I was grandly presented with a large bunch of flowers. I did not really care. I was back where I always wanted to be—in front of an appreciative audience. It may have been a long way from the West End, where I could have starred as an actress, and even further from La Scala, Milan, where I had dreamed of starring as a singer, but I felt alive again.

Mr Salberg and the management of the Grand Theatre were obviously pleased by the audience's reaction to the short experimental repertory season, and it was decided the company should stay on a long-term basis. I was offered a permanent job and I am quite sure some of my smart London friends would have been horrified at the alacrity with which I accepted. They were always sympathizing with me for having to stay in the provinces, but while it was true that I sometimes missed the bright lights of the metropolis, I was happy enough in Wolverhampton.

I was to stay with the company at the Grand for fourteen years and during that time I played dozens of different roles in all sorts of productions. If I say so myself, I became quite good as an actress who specialized in character and comedy roles, once I got my sense of fun back.

When the war started, we were rehearsing for a play called *The Queen Was in the Parlour* and I think it was the cancelling of the production and the closing of the theatre that really brought home to me just how serious the situation had become. Before then it was just something one heard about on the wireless or read about in the newspapers. Once the war began, everyone wanted to do their bit and I volunteered and was accepted as a part-time ambulance-driver. It was the best I could do because I was frightened of the memories that any attempt at nursing might bring back.

I did not do a great deal of ambulance-driving, because after only a week or so the theatre reopened—with a production of *Home and Away*—when it was decided that there was still a need for some form of entertainment for war workers and troops on leave. Things were, of course, much different to peacetime days. We stumbled through the black-out to the theatre and then had to dash off at the end of the performances to catch the last buses, because petrol-rationing meant few could run private cars. Members of the company kept disappearing as call-up papers arrived and the men went off to join the army, navy or air force. For those of us who stayed behind, there was a kind of frenetic need to pretend that all was normal—business as usual—the show must go on—and most of the time I think we succeeded.

I have to confess that I was almost enjoying life again. But I never lost my caution, I was always aware that disaster could be just over the next hill. I kept my little shop, although it was hard work being there during the day and going on stage at night. And I fell in love again, twice, and both times with married men. I did not know the first was married until after we got engaged. This was at the beginning of the war and I suppose he found it easy to operate under camouflage. I could not believe it when I finally found out he already had a wife and all his talk of love was just a lot of rubbish. I think my anger helped me overcome the hurt. Most of the anger was, of course, directed at myself for being so gullible, but that disaster did not stop me falling in love for a third time. This time I did know the man was married, but I believed him when he told me that the relationship between him and his wife had been shaky long before I arrived on the scene. He was an actor and so we used to see a lot of each other around the theatre. He was very gentle and sensitive and although I knew it was all very silly, I could not help loving him. When he told me he loved me, I think it was actually true and I feel that, with encouragement, he would have left his wife to marry me. I, however, got very frightened, probably by the thought of an embarrassing divorce case. I was well known in Wolverhampton and it would almost certainly have been in all the papers, and there is no telling how that would have affected my parents and younger brother. Divorce was still a scandal

45

in those days. Anyway, screwing up all my courage, I broke off the relationship and never saw him again. He died shortly afterwards. So even if I had stayed with him, I still would not have become a bride. I felt that third time unlucky meant I was not destined to be married, and that is the point where romance and I went our separate ways. I accepted that I was going to be what was sniggeringly called an old maid, and determined to go on making some kind of success out of my business and my still-flourishing stage career.

Yellowing press cuttings are no real substitute for a wedding album, but I really have had a great deal of pleasure over the years from poring over some of the notices I received for my stage performances:

Murder on the Second Floor—Gwen Berryman, of course, had a part after her own heart in the boarding-house keeper, and she played it with her usual skill, extracting every ounce of humour from the character and the situation.

You Asked for It—From the opening chorus, in which she sings 'I'm in by Weight', Gwen Berryman could not put a foot wrong. Neither her invaluable training as a singer, nor her sense of humour in the self-mocking way she emphasized her own plumpness, were lost on an enthusiastic audience.

Cockpit—The Alexandra Theatre was so cleverly converted into a displaced persons' transit camp that I thought for a moment the task of subduing the mob, of which the audience was now a part, was going to be too much for Gwen Berryman. But subdue us she did . . . and in an enchanging way . . . with a beautifully performed song.

I was in probably one hundred and fifty different plays and revues during those fourteen years, mainly at the Grand Theatre, Wolverhampton, but also in various parts of the Midlands; and I might well have gone on to do hundreds more if I had not once more found myself in circumstances where my career had to take a back-seat. My mother became very ill and needed much more attention that I could have given had I gone on being a stage actress.

I never resented having to give up my work because my parents had done so much for me and I saw looking after Mum as a small repayment for all their sacrifices over the years. Mum had not really approved when I abandoned my operatic career and instead went on the stage. But, no doubt as much to please my father as much as anything else, she never uttered one word of criticism and in fact grew to enjoy her regular visits to the Grand to see me perform. We often talked about the theatre as

47

she lay on her sickbed and she was, I think, very upset that she should be keeping me from acting.

I thought I was going into a kind of temporary retirement but in fact I was just edging towards a new emphasis to my career. I had appeared on the wireless once or twice when I was still a singing student at the Birmingham School of Music in 1926 (my first fee was seven shillings and sixpence or a free dinner and I took the free dinner!), but until after the war I had not done any acting on the air. Now I began to get one or two offers and because it meant just the odd day here and there, I was able to accept them.

The first major production I was booked for was a twelve-part serialization of Arnold Bennet's *The Old Wives' Tale*. That is, of course, set in the Potteries, North Staffordshire, and I suspect the BBC producer did not quite know the difference between that accent and my own, which was South Staffordshire. Anyway, I found myself in the company of Mary Wimbush and Marjorie Westbury, two of the great ladies of radio; Valentine Dyall, who I think will always be labelled 'The Man in Black' for all those wonderful stories he read at bedtime; and another actor from Wolverhampton, one Chris Gittins, who was later to become Walter Gabriel. This was in July, 1948, and the programme was broadcast live on the Midland Home Service. I enjoyed the experience so much that I was determined to try to make something of this new opportunity. I knew I had not got the Potteries accent quite right when I started, so I used to nip up to Stoke-on-Trent whenever I could. There I just travelled on the buses, listened to the locals, until I had perfected the accent and the dialect. That was a trick Mabel Constandurous had taught me many years earlier when I needed to acquire a Cockney voice for *Derby Day*. It certainly paid off because I was subsequently top of the list whenever Midland accents were needed. In another Arnold Bennett play, *The Card*, I played opposite Wilfred Pickles and then, in 1950, Leslie Halward wrote a play specially for me. It was called *Mom*, and really it just centred around one day in the life of an ordinary Midland family. He said he devised it for me because I was always complaining that parts for middle-aged actresses—I was then forty-four—were usually only peripheral to the play. In *Mom*, I was involved throughout the forty-five minutes and never worked so hard in my life, but it was exhilarating and very, very flattering. My husband, incidentally, was played by Eddie Robinson, who also came from Wolverhampton, and who would also become a regular in Ambridge. My son was the young John Neville.

It was very shortly afterwards that I was introduced to Doris Archer, in a letter from

Godfrey Baseley:

Dear Mrs Berryman, You may have heard that after Christmas there's a possibility of a daily serial play (The Archers) coming from the Midland Region, on similar lines to that of *Mrs Dale's Diary*.

There are still one or two parts not yet cast for this and I wondered whether you would care to come into Birmingham on 3 November, at 5.10 pm to give me an audition for the part of Mrs Archer. I'm enclosing a few details about this character in order that you may be prepared to some extent.

I'm arranging for a special scene to be written for the audition, in which you will play opposite one or two of the characters already cast.

For your information, if you are eventually selected for the part, it would mean recording the five episodes during Saturday, Sunday and Monday morning of each week, and a contract would be issued to cover the thirteen weeks to the end of March.

Perhaps you'd let me know if you are interested in this.

I had obviously played so many married women that Godfrey must have assumed that I was actually *Mrs* Berryman, and I often wondered whether or not I would even have been offered an audition if he had realized that I was a Miss! Certainly he seemed to have very positive ideas of what kind of character he wanted, and I really did not think that was me from the pen portrait he enclosed with his letter.

Mrs Archer is aged somewhere round about fifty-five. She is a farmer's wife on a smallish farm. Her past history is as follows:

She was a daughter of a gamekeeper and went to the village school until she was fourteen, then she went into service at the Manor House, proved herself to be trustworthy and capable and developed through the various grades until she became a personal lady's maid to the daughter of the house. She had, by this time, acquired a good knowledge of what you might call 'good manners and behaviour'. She then married Daniel Archer, who was working with his father on a small farm. His father died fairly soon after they were married and Daniel took over the farm. They had a very hard struggle to begin with, through years of depression, but they managed to carry on and Mrs Archer had, during this period, three children—Jack, Philip and Christine.

Jack, the eldest, was only able to have an elementary school education. As times improved, Philip was able to satisfy something of his mother's ambition for him by passing an examination to the county grammar school, and from there on to an agricultural college by the skin of his teeth. Christine, who was younger than the boys, was able to have a better start in life by then, by virtue of more prosperity to the farm. She was quite bright and the play will open with her on the point of leaving school, after passing Higher School Certificate.

You may gather from this that Mrs Archer is ambitious, and I think that what she's trying to do is to copy in some way what was done at the Manor for the children there. She has a certain amount of pride, is a good and thorough housewife, tolerant with her husband, who is perhaps a little old-fashioned, but able to understand and appreciate to some degree the ways of youth in a modern world. I don't want the character to have any accent at all, but I want her to be recognized as a country woman in her manner and speech.

Godfrey was being less than gallant in guessing at the lady's age—she was actually only fifty—but then one should remember he had only known her for a short time at that point, and it is not until you start to add flesh to the bones that you begin to see her real personality.

While my father was working his apprenticeship in the grime of Wolverhampton, Doris's father was out in all weathers learning to be a gamekeeper. Both were clearly decent, hard-working youths, but while one could dream of becoming his own master, the other—

the young countryman—could only accept the near-feudal servility to his elders and betters. He may not have actually had to tug his forelock, but William Forrest was never under any illusions about his future—he would do exactly as he was told, when he was told and he would do his damnedest to do a good day's work. His rewards, he knew, would be a clean, comfortable bed and a full belly, plus as much knowledge about the countryside and its flora and fauna as his mind could absorb. It should not be imagined that there was any less spirit in a young man who knew his place in the rural society. Young Bill always did what he thought was right for the land, even if that did not appear to suit the landowner. A mutual respect developed between Bill and his master, a respect that might not readily be apparent to the outsider. When he decided to marry he moved out of the staff quarters at the big house and into a tiny cottage provided for him and his new bride, Lisa, by the squire. Life was hard for the young couple, with Bill working long hours for what an industrial worker would have regarded as a pittance.

The Forrests had only been married for a year or so when their first child was born, on 11 July, 1900. It was a girl and she was christened Doris, in the village church, before a congregation that was so perfectly rural that it could have been created by Thomas Hardy for one of his Wessex tales. Christmas that year was good for the Forrests—Bill had just been promoted to senior keeper—and they were too happy to be aware of the meagreness of their weekly wage or of their lack of creature comforts.

Within the year Lisa again found herself pregnant and on 10 January 1902, she had a son, Edward George. Seemingly as a reward for that—or it could have been because Bill was doing well in his more responsible job—the family was moved to a bigger cottage on the estate. The extra space did little to add to the physical comfort of the Forrests, but to Lisa in particular it did represent progress and, although all but imperceptible, a move up the well-defined country social ladder. It was unlikely that the squire and his lady would drop in for afternoon tea, but now the head keeper would sometimes call for a glass of ale and if the estate factor had occasion to call, he would accept the invitation to step inside rather than give his instructions on the doorstep.

When she was old enough, little Doris went to the village school and made her first, stumbling attempts to read and write under the disciplinarian eye of Miss Brammidge. She was not especially bright and even had the opportunities been there, it is doubtful if she would have aspired to the glittering prizes. But there were not the chances, and the little girl simply learned what she could, unaware of any world beyond Ambridge. Doris, her little brother, Ted, and a second brother, Tom (who was born when Doris was ten), were victims of circumstances, born into an almost closed society, in which they would spend their whole lives. Not for them my ambition to become a great performer on the world stage.

When Doris left school at the age of thirteen, the only thing for her to do was to go into service. But she was luckier than most—because of her father's position—and she was taken on at the big house, working for the squire of Ambridge. Vacancies there were few and far between and the alternative would have been to go away from home and be a living-in servant elsewhere.

Doris started off as a kitchen maid and she always retained bitter-sweet memories of those Edwardian days. She used to get up at the crack of dawn, to walk—whatever the weather—over the fields to the big house. Once there, she had to do all the donkey work before the cook would deign to prepare breakfast for the household. It was a hard life for a thirteen-year-old girl. At an age when I was swanning around school, plotting a starry future from my comfortable middle-class baseline, Doris was scrubbing floors, cleaning out fireplaces, washing dishes and jumping every time one of her 'betters' wanted anything doing. But, Doris being Doris, she seldom recalled that side of her job without

55

also talking about the thrill of seeing the landed gentry celebrating the traditional English events like harvest and Christmas; the tables laden with food, wine and ale flowing fast, and handsome men and the elegant ladies. It was a glimpse of a beautiful world, at least as she saw it. It was, of course, a world that a poor country girl could never join.

Both Doris's brothers followed her into the squire's employ, both, like their father, becoming gamekeepers. It never worried them that they lived in a tied-cottage and that their whole existence was so absolutely in the hands of one man. Squire Lawson-Hope was a good man, as far as they were concerned, and they saw him as much as a provider as a master.

Tragedy first entered Doris's life not long after her twentieth birthday, when her young brother Ted was killed in a shooting accident on the estate. But country folk seem more able to accept these kinds of things and she was spared most of the terrible distress that shattered me when my fiancé died. She had her period of grief and mourning and then there was work that had to be done, a life that had to go on.

By now, Doris had become lady's maid to the squire's wife and was beginning to catch the eye of the village lads—and she responded to one of them in particular, Dan Archer, who was about four years older than her. Dan was the eldest of three brothers who all worked for their father, tenant of Brookfield Farm. The youngest boy, Frank, seeing little hope of progress in Ambridge, emigrated to New Zealand, and when the First World War started Dan and the other brother, John, enlisted in the army. John was posted to the front, but just before Dan was due to follow him, their father became seriously ill. As the eldest son, Dan was expected to return home to run the farm, and he was discharged from the army on compassionate grounds. Just after he got back, his father died and Dan, still not twenty-one, was left to run Brookfield single-handed.

It was during this period that Dan and Doris started 'walking out' together, and everyone in the village assumed that they would eventually marry. Brother John's return from the war—to a hero's welcome—nearly changed all that. Rather than knuckling down to work alongside Dan, he spent most of his time gallivanting around the country, taking advantage of his heroic status, especially with the girls. At first Dan was understanding and, possibly because he felt guilty about not having gone to the front, did not press the younger lad to help. Then discontent began to smoulder and it was fanned by the attention John started paying Doris. Although he had not actually asked her to marry him, Dan's intentions were pretty obvious to everyone. But John ignored all that and carried on flirting with her. Things came to a head on the Christmas night, when the brothers had spent the day with the Forrest family. Dan saw John catch Doris under the mistletoe and it was too much for him. When they got back to Brookfield, he decided to have it out with him, brother or no brother.

Bitter words were hurled around and all Dan's frustration about the younger man's laziness poured out. It soon became clear that Brookfield was not big enough for both of them. One of them would have to leave. But who? They agreed that the only way to settle it was physically. There and then, despite Christmas and the season of goodwill, the two shaped up to each other in the barn at Brookfield.

It was a tough, brutal battle with neither sparing any effort to hurt the other. In the end it was the older brother, Dan, who was still standing. He was bruised and bleeding, but John was in an even worse state and as he lay there on the floor of the barn, Dan made him confirm his promise that, as the loser, he would leave Brookfield and Ambridge. Next morning, when Dan got back from tending the stock, the farmhouse was empty. John had kept his promise and had left.

Doris knew little about this incident for many years. She saw Dan as a rather gentle character but one with a steely determination that would give him the courage to fight all the odds that nature stacks against any young man trying to build up a farm. And she loved him.

They married in December, 1921, just a few months after Doris's twenty-first birthday. Dan was twenty-five. They set up home at Brookfield, and for the first time Doris was her own mistress.

It was not a way of life for the weak. If doing scullery chores in the big house was hard, being a farmer's chief cook, bottle-washer and labourer—at a time when there were no mechanical aids on the farm and no electronic gadgets in the farmhouse—was almost as tough as doing hard labour in a chain gang. It was remorseless toil, seven days a week, fifty-two weeks a year. The livestock didn't recognize high days or holidays and a farmer's wife was expected to share the responsibility of tending and feeding them.

How women in that situation found time to bring up a family is something I can only marvel at; but for Doris, having two sons (Jack and Philip) and a daughter (Christine) simply meant adding another role to her already long list of responsibilities. She accepted as normal a life anyone else would have regarded as incredibly hectic. In fact, she even managed to find time to be involved in the social life of the village. One of the few things she and I shared was a love for singing. Obviously she did not have any opportunities for training her voice, as I did, but she and Dan were good enough to provide really good entertainment with their duets at village socials, some of which she organized herself. One other thing we had in common was cooking, her enthusiasm growing out of a need to feed hungry mouths, mine from simple enjoyment of creating new recipes.

So that was Doris Archer as she was in 1950, when Godfrey Baseley first introduced her in his letter. We did not have much in common, I thought, but she seemed a very nice lady. It was only in later years that we were to develop common characteristics.

CHAPTER THREE

As instructed so precisely in the letter, I sat nervously outside the drama studio at the BBC's Midland Region centre in Broad Street, Birmingham, just before 5.10 pm on Friday, 3 November, 1950. I was as nervous as a kitten because I desperately wanted the part and I knew there were at least seven other actresses being seen. I had also been told that the woman who had appeared in a trial run had been dropped because she did not have the right accent.

I was the fourth to be shown into the studio at almost exactly 5.10, and I think the apparent efficiency of the operation unsettled me even further. There were four men on the audition panel and the only one I knew reasonably well was Tony Shryane, who had been studio manager on *The Card*. The others were Edward J. Mason and Geoffrey Webb, the writers, who I had never seen before, and Godfrey Baseley, whom I had only seen around the BBC canteen.

Tony Shryane, who was then about thirty, was a nice man whom I had enjoyed working with and who tried, although the most junior of the four, to make me feel less nervous. All I can remember of Ted Mason then was that he had crinkly eyes and a little goatee beard. Geoff Webb seemed enormous—in fact he was six feet two inches tall, but as gentle as a lamb. Godfrey Baseley was obviously in charge. Slightly balding, with horn-rimmed glasses and a floppy bow tie, he talked with alarming precision and very positive authority. Actually, he frightened the life out of me, as he explained what was expected of me: 'Read this script as if you were president of the WI; this as if you were talking to your husband out in the farmyard; and this as if you were on the telephone to an old friend.'

He also gave me information about not using an accent but sounding like a country woman, about moving my voice up and down the register and not letting it get too light—at least, I think that was what he was saying because the truth is that I really did not understand what I was supposed to do. Anyway, all I could do was to try. I did—and he was not happy; I did again—and he was not happy; I did yet again—and he still was not happy; and on, and on, and on. I think we went through the procedure sixteen times in all, although Tony Shryane later tried to convince me that it was not quite that bad.

One of the problems, I discovered later, was that because all the other parts had already been filled (during the trial), they were trying to match my voice to that of the other actresses. Anyway, at the end of the session I felt like a wet rag, and I swear that if Godfrey Baseley had offered me the part—or even the Crown Jewels—just at that moment, I would have told him to go and jump in the river! He did not, of course, and I was allowed to stumble off into the night to have a thoroughly miserable weekend. Most of the following week was pretty awful too, and by the time the BBC letter dropped on to my doormat, I could not bear to open it. Luckily my brother Trevor was in the house at the time and I got him to read it first.

I cannot honestly say that I was overjoyed by what should have been good news—the offer to play the part of Doris. I was still very scared of Godfrey Baseley and I was not sure that I would be able to work for him. I also had a sneaking feeling that he did not want me for the part. He had said several times during the audition that he really wanted an older voice than mine. I was sensitive enough not to want to work with anyone who did not want me. Like any actress, I wanted to be loved by everybody.

I decided that I would turn down the offer.

However, before I had plucked up the courage to tell the BBC, I learned that Godfrey was not going to produce the programme. Although he was to be in overall charge, his other responsibilities prevented him being in the studio as much as would be needed and Tony Shryane was to be the producer. What a relief, and I promptly changed my mind and graciously, I think, accepted the usual BBC terms.

The first contract for The Archers arrived at my home on 23 November—it was my forty-fourth birthday!

Less than a fortnight later I was back at the Broad Street studio to meet the other members of the cast and record the first five episodes of The Archers, which would then start to go out on the Light Programme on New Year's Day. There were nine of us: me, Harry Oakes (Dan), Norman Painting (Philip), June Spencer (Peggy), Denis Folwell (Jack), Pamela Mant (Christine), Monica Grey (Grace), Robert Mawdesley (Walter) and Eddie Robinson (Simon). All the others knew each other from having been in the trial run earlier in the year but I had only worked before with Harry (who, it later transpired, was the person who had

63

suggested me for the part of Doris) and Eddie Robinson, who also came from Wolverhampton. It was not really like a family gathering; it was much too hard work for that. We had just two days to do all five episodes, which meant about three hours for each programme. There were no editing facilities then, because the recordings were made direct on to enormous discs, so if anyone made a mistake or even left too much of a pause, we had to go right back to the beginning again. Of course, in radio you do have the advantage of reading off the script so there is no chance of forgetting lines or not being too sure when to come into a conversation.

I cannot remember whether or not it went particularly smoothly, but at the end of the last episode we all heaved a great sigh of relief when Tony Shryane pronounced his satisfaction. He later told me that, from his point of view, the whole production worked like a dream and he was really thrilled. It was his first experience as a producer!

So much had already been written about how the programme was conceived and what the initial premise was that I do not feel any need to go all over that again, except, perhaps, to repeat that everyone did seem to believe that it was only going to last three months. One or two people have subsequently said they had a hunch that it was going to be a success and last much longer than that. I was not one of those who had such perception. To me, still quite new to the wireless, it was just a really good job which would give me tremendous exposure on the Light Programme (until then, my few plays had been broadcast on the Home Service) and I was absolutely thrilled to have been given such a long run. I certainly did not think beyond the promised three months. In any case, there had been a bit of a row over the signature tune and that had only helped to underline our impermanence. Godfrey Baseley had wanted to have specially-composed music played by a big orchestra, but that would have cost more than £250 and his bosses did not think it was worth that kind of money for a short run. We had to make do with an existing tune on a gramophone record, though that happened to be 'Barwick Green' which, of course, has survived until this day.

When I heard the first episode go out that New Year's Day, I felt quite pleased with myself. I fitted in well with the others and, knowing two or three farmers' wives myself, I thought I sounded the part. As well as that, we had all succeeded in not falling into the pit dug for the unwary venturing into rural characterization—the Mummerset accent. Mind you, I'm not too sure what I thought about Walter Gabriel's voice. It was, perhaps, a bit too ripe for my taste, but it soon became a firm favourite with the listeners.

I have read in various books and articles about The Archers that the programme was an overnight success. If it was, no one bothered to tell me, or, as far as I know, anyone else in the cast. Actors and actresses are notoriously insecure and in the first few weeks we were more or less left to stew in our own juice. Of course, lots of my friends and relatives said how much they enjoyed listening to the programme and they all dutifully told me how good I was as Doris, but none of that counted because we are more or less geared to receiving false praise from kindly people.

In fact, the first inkling I personally had that more than Mum and Dad and some of the customers at my shop in Wolverhampton were beginning to listen regularly was when letters began to arrive from different parts of the country, and that was about a month after we went on the air. The first official indication of success came after that when the BBC one day asked us to dress up for our parts. It was not for the recordings—although lots of people did think that we performed 'in costume' on radio—but for a special publicity-photograph session. The press and magazines, including the BBC's own *Radio Times*, were taking a keen interest in The Archers and it seemed there was a constant clamour for pictures.

Godfrey Baseley, I know, was very much

against having any photographs taken and initially he resisted all the pressures. He, understandably, did not want to shatter any of the illusions that he had so carefully created for the radio listeners. He insisted that each of us had been chosen purely and simply because of our voices and he had seen it as his job to blend those voices into a general picture, leaving the listeners to fill in the details themselves. The response to the programme had been such, he said, that he had obviously succeeded in stimulating the imagination. Putting faces to the voices would interfere with listeners' own ideas of what we all looked like and that would wreck all his careful plans.

One had to have sympathy with his argument, after all, how would people react to the fact that Jack was a couple of years older than his mother? And that was what they would see from a photograph of Denis Folwell, who played Jack, and me, as Doris.

Whether or not Godfrey changed his mind or was overruled by somebody higher up the BBC pyramid I don't know, but in the end photographs were taken and began to appear in dozens of newspapers and magazines. As it happened, with the one exception of Denis, the rest of the original cast did look more or less the right ages and, if you did not study the poses too closely, we all passed muster as country characters. Mind you, if anyone had actually asked Robert Mawdesley to do anything with the pitchfork he wielded on behalf of Walter Gabriel, I dread to think what might have happened!

Although success was now quite clearly in the air, still no one said anything about extending the promised three months' run. I am sure someone somewhere must have been thinking about it, but I suspect they did not think members of the cast were important enough to discuss such matters. Then, quite suddenly, we were all offered further contracts that would take us through to the end of June. Good news is worth waiting for. And there was more to come—a schedule change was planned. Such BBC jargon meant little to me but it was interpreted for me by a friendly secretary: The Archers was to be broadcast at quarter-to-seven in the evening, instead of quarter-to-twelve in the morning, and that meant the end of *Dick Barton, Special Agent*. I do not think I was told why all this was to happen, but it was obviously a good thing, because by the end of the first week at the new time, the audience was reported to have doubled to around four million. Now, as the fan letters started to pour in, the talk of success became more insistent and everyone seemed to be anxious to analyse the programme's attraction for the listeners and equally anxious to establish their part in it. I must have done *my* bit, but honestly, browsing through some of the early scripts, I could not tell you how. I seemed to be forever doing housework and cooking breakfast, with such contributions to the dialogue as:

'You sit down. I'll get the toast.'
'D'you want one egg or two?'
'Not until after breakfast.'
'Your breakfast's on the table now!'
'Your breakfast'll get cold if you don't hurry!'
'Dan! Breakfast.'
'Philip your breakfast ... you've hardly started it.'

But if I was not overburdened with the need to learn and interpret long speeches, I was getting the chance to really work myself into my characterization and to breathe life into the two-dimensional Doris Archer. And that was happening to others in the cast too. In one of the newspapers at the time, Godfrey Baseley was quoted as saying: 'There's no doubt about it, we're all caught up in country fever and I've never known a group of actors and actresses get so caught up in the parts they play.' He was quite right, it was beginning to feel very different from any of my previous plays for radio, but I suspect egotism had as much to do with it as country fever. You see, as the writers were getting to know us, they were beginning to reflect bits of our real personalities in writing our Archer characters, and quite a lot of our natural speech patterns were also working their way into the programme. For example, once it was realized that both Harry Oakes and I were singers, so Dan and Doris began to sing happily together, both at home and at village concerts and things. It was there, I suppose, that the subsequent blurring of fact and fiction had its roots.

There were other things which also made confusion the more likely. The dressing up for photographs became the norm—the number of times I had to wear one of those wrap-around pinnies and roll up my sleeves! (One photographer said that rolling up the sleeves was very important because it was the plumpness of my elbows that proved I really was a country wife. I hadn't the heart to tell him that I was *Miss* Berryman from darkest Wolverhampton.) We also started doing recordings outside the studio and so we would find ourselves playing out our story in a real church, perhaps, with the real congregation all around us, or in a real pub with its own regulars providing the background noise, and with the cast, of course, dressed for our parts.

Any actor will tell you that there's nothing like putting on the right clothes and being in the right setting to help you develop the character you are supposed to be. Neither of these things usually happened in radio drama and the fact that they now were for us must have been a big help, although I do not think we realized it at the time. Nor did we notice that the cast was beginning to grow together just like a family and we soon found ourselves always sitting in the same chairs in the Green Room between recordings, and always around the same tables in the BBC canteen. We were establishing our territorial rights!

We were also becoming stars. There is no other word for it. By the end of our first year on the air the daily listening-figure had grown to six million and we had outstripped *Mrs Dale's Diary*, to become one of the biggest attractions on British radio. Just what an achievement that was can be seen from the way this fact was reported in the national press.

Mrs Dale's Diary, for years the BBC's top daily serial, has been pushed into second place by the family farming programme, The Archers. This BBC secret was revealed by the Midland Region last night—to the surprise of the London HQ, for listener figures, compiled by the research unit, are usually given only to one hundred and twenty BBC heads of departments. Now, says the Midland Region, six million a day listen to The Archers. 'This means they have exceeded the Dale figure by about a million,' adds the Midland announcement.

The Archers *is* a Midland serial, but is so good that it gets a daily national broadcast with an omnibus edition on Saturdays. *Mrs Dale's Diary* is a London programme with a daily national broadcast.

When the omnibus edition mentioned in the report began in early 1952, we gained another three million regular listeners and now no one bothered to speculate how long the programme might last, we just carried on, and on, and on.

Being stars, we were also in great demand for public appearances all over the country and although many of the invitations were to all of us, others were to Harry Oakes and myself as a couple. We were, however, quite different from the other popular entertainers of the day. We were seldom seen as actors, nearly always we were described as Dan, Doris, Walter or whatever, and we were lucky if our own names were added in brackets.

All this helped us to get to know each other very well and we developed close friendships within the cast. For example, I became great chums with Harry Oakes and his real wife, Dorothy. The three of us travelled all over the country and had some marvellous times together with Harry, a great practical joker and natural comic, always proudly showing off his two wives. Because of the similarity of names—he called his wife Dot—he would occasionally get muddled up. But there was never any real confusion, no identity crises for Dorothy or me.

Harry, a townie like me, was from the Potteries, and again like me had never really set out to become an actor. He was trained as a commercial artist and worked for many years painting and designing china crockery. He got the show business bug when he joined the army, in the First World War, and was pressed into taking part in the forces shows. When he got back to Stoke-on-Trent, he joined the local amateur dramatic society and spent much of his spare time acting, singing and even dancing. He did not turn professional for many years and in fact he had done his first radio drama only a year or so before he joined The Archers.

Wherever we went, Harry always kept us in stitches. He hated driving and allocated the chauffeur's role to Dorothy, but then he made up for that with a constant stream of amusing conversation and entertainment. He was a great limerick man and one that sticks in my memory he made up as we drove through a little place near Market Harborough in Leicestershire.

There was a young lady of Lubenham,
　　Couldn't dance on her toes without
　　　　stubbin' 'em,
So she tied all her toes first in knots, then in
　　bows,
　　Then bought embrocation for rubbin' 'em.

We would also practise our singing as we bowled along and I am sure people must have sometimes thought we were mad. Because of my opera training, I think I had a better voice than Harry (who had only taken singing lessons as part of his stage craft) and I always enjoyed showing off with snatches from arias that he could not cope with. Mind you, I may have been a bit too clever, because whenever we had to sing together as Dan and Doris on the programme, Tony Shryane always complained that I sounded too professional and asked me to try to avoid singing in the correct key!

Harry and I would also take advantage of being together in the car to rehearse our scripted conversations and that meant by the time we went into the studio we had already been through all the possible interpretations of the dialogue and were able to give what appeared to some of the others as instant performances.

The popularity of the programme intensified and the fan mail increased in volume. If we had not been so busy keeping up with all the promotion work and enjoying all the adulation, we might have been worried by the degree of identification some listeners were building up with the fictional characters. I was always being asked for recipes, cooking tips and advice on how to cope with family problems and it was clear that many of the letter-writers believed they were in touch with Doris Archer, rather than an actress playing a part. Denis Folwell was always being told off whenever Jack appeared less than capable as a husband and father; Robert Mawdesley was sent cures for Walter's various ailments; Monica Grey was warned that she (Grace) should not marry Philip (Norman Painting) because he was not good enough for her; Eddie Robinson was offered a farm-labourer's job when Dan was being unpleasant with Simon, his farm-hand; and at Christmas time, we got orders for turkeys (some of them enclosing postal orders) addressed to Brookfield Farm!

Just why this should happen, none of us really knew; we were all simply delighted with our new-found fame (or notoriety in one or two cases). One of the contributory factors, looking back, must have been Tony Shryane's style of producing the programme. I remember one of his first directions was that the dialogue was to be not so much heard as overheard. His theory was that if you gave the impression that you were speaking for the listeners' benefit, they *might* listen, if what you were saying was very interesting. But let them imagine that they were only overhearing a conversation and they would hang on every word. He said he wanted an audience of eavesdroppers, and all the evidence of those early days suggested that he was getting one. By the one-hundredth episode, Godfrey

Baseley was able to write in *Radio Times*: 'Already in this short space of time the family has established itself as a firm favourite with a vast listening audience.'

In the same article Godfrey said one of the programme's attractions was that every detail of the rural life it portrayed, was authentic: 'Whether the script deals with actual farming, market gardening, the activities of the WI or conversation in the local pub, it is tested and retested for accuracy and truth to life.' While that was certainly true as far as the scripts went, I could not help smiling when I looked around the studio at the members of the cast—where was the authenticity here? Harry Oakes and myself I have already labelled—perhaps exposed might be a better word—as out-and-out townies. It was true that Robert Mawdesley lived in the country, somewhere in the Cotswolds, but any similarity between him and Walter Gabriel ended right there. Bob was a Cambridge graduate, ex-RAF and a former announcer for the BBC. His own natural voice was beautifully modulated and it is hard to imagine anything more different than Walter's wheezy, rasping rumbustiousness. June Spencer and Denis Folwell were also a far cry from the characters of Peggy (a cockney ex-ATS girl) and Jack (a struggling small-holder). June was very much a Midlander—from Nottingham—and had never been near the ATS. Her career had been in the theatre. Denis, an ex-army officer and former theatre producer, did not really know the difference between a small-holding and an allotment. Norman Painting, who played my other son, Philip, was closer to the land than that—he lived in a converted barn. But born in Leamington Spa, an Anglo-Saxon scholar and former BBC producer, writer and reporter, he had nothing in common with young Philip Archer. The only one of us to have any kind of similar interests to the character she played was Pamela Mant. Like Christine in the programme, Pamela was a keen horsewoman and she did in fact live in the country—actually in the middle of a field, where she had a lovely old gypsy caravan.

Brookfield Farm, too, was an amazing cheat. Whatever listeners might have imagined, it was a small, box-like studio, two floors above a motor-car showroom, right in the middle of Birmingham. Of course, we had to learn our way round that studio just as if it were Brookfield. There were different positions for the kitchen, the yard, the cowsheds, and we even had the bar at The Bull in there. I remember the telephone was supposed to be in the hall at the farmhouse, but it was in fact in the corner of the studio just under the clock, with the kitchen sink on the opposite wall. And all the doors, hatches and gates of Ambridge were contained in a couple of moveable structures fitted with dozens of locks, latches and catches. While Doris was able to make and serve a cup of tea in the comfort of her kitchen, our reality was that we had to send the programme secretary, Valerie Hodgetts, off on a route march whenever we wanted anything. The canteen was at the opposite end of the building and the only way to get to it was down the stairs, into the main street, along past the car showroom (which was just opposite the Bingley Hall) and into a separate entrance. One day, Valerie had made the trek and collected a tray laden with more than a dozen cups and saucers and two enormous pots of coffee. Just as she came out of the canteen, a nearby clock started to strike eleven o'clock. It was Armistice Day. All the traffic stopped, every pedestrian stood still, and for two very long minutes, in complete silence, the poor girl held the heavy tray with her arms aching. I think she felt as if she had milked a thousand cows by the time she staggered back into the studio.

However unrealistic that might all have been, once inside that studio we shed our real personalities. Godfrey Baseley and Tony Shryane always used our character names when we were at the microphone and that, of course, was what the listeners heard—Dan and Doris in their farmhouse in Ambridge, in the heart of rural England.

CHAPTER FOUR

By the end of the first year, the programme's success was no longer in question. It had established a real grip on the audience and that ended all the speculation about how long it might go on. Now there was a tacit assumption that The Archers was here to stay for the foreseeable future. Mind you, for members of the cast, all we were allowed to foresee was three months, because the BBC would not let us have contracts for any longer than that. Apart from all the usual theatrical neuroticism, we were actually very happy with that arrangement. The truth is that three months is an awful lot longer than the majority of actors ever have.

During the year, the cast increased in size as the writers introduced some of the other residents of Ambridge, and I, for example, discovered that my new family included a brother—Tom Forrest—who was the local gamekeeper. As the numbers grew, so the writers also were able to flesh out the characters and I found myself getting to know quite a lot about Doris Archer.

At this distance in time, I cannot honestly be sure what my feelings were about her, but I do not think she was exactly my favourite person. For a start, she really was very nosey and seemed to know about everyone else's business around the village. She did not have much of a sense of humour and my goodness but she nagged her poor husband something shocking! Now, I'm not the gossipy, inquisitive type and I *do* have a sense of humour that's often been my only salvation in difficult situations, so I am quite sure that if she had been a real person, we would not have been the best of friends.

Like her or not, however, she was very important to my career, giving me lots of work and a good, steady income (of about ten pounds a week when the programme started), and I worked hard at developing her character. As I mentioned before, I did have one or two friends who were farmers' wives and I chatted to them as often as possible about the problems of bringing up a family on a busy farm. I even went as far as keeping a couple of pigs at the bottom of my garden in Wolverhampton so that I could make my own pork pies, just as she might have done. I don't think I had much difficulty with persuading listeners that I sounded like a country-woman, and when it came to all the photographs and public appearances, my figure and my cheerful-looking face helped me actually to look the part of the farmer's wife.

It was the public appearances that made me aware of how much pleasure people got from listening to The Archers and it was that in turn that gave me my greatest pleasure in being part of the programme. Without that contact, I do not think I would have stayed on playing Doris Archer as long as I did. You see, although it was nearly always quite pleasant working in the studio with people like Harry Oakes and June Spencer, the recording schedule was relentless and whenever Godfrey Baseley was around, he was so demanding, he made me feel that The Archers was the only thing that mattered to him and that, somehow, I was letting him down by not sharing his obsession. Godfrey and I had many rows because I let my life outside the studio interfere. I wanted time off to look after my mother when she was ill, for example, and to have longer than the regular fortnight's holiday. Such needs seemed to be beyond his comprehension and I often dissolved helplessly into tears. In fact, there were at least three or four occasions when I was so upset that I resigned. It was usually Tony Shryane or Norman Painting who calmed me down and persuaded me to carry on. Really, I am ever so grateful to them.

Of course, I am very, very grateful to Godfrey too. Despite all the aggravation, I do recognize that he was the driving force behind The Archers and I now know that it was his energy and enthusiasm that kept everyone going when things got tough. I just wish that every now and then he could have been a bit less dogmatic, a bit more charming, and an awful lot less rude!

In contrast to Godfrey, the people I met during our public appearances were almost always kind and considerate. As the programme developed, the invitations to various events multiplied at an amazing rate and we found ourselves travelling the length and breadth of the land. In those early days, we opened garden fêtes, handed out school prizes, crowned carnival queens, visited stately homes, toured factories, kicked-off soccer matches, judged flower shows. And everywhere, we gave speeches, posed for photographs, shook hands and signed autographs. This was no touring sideshow: we were always the main attraction. It fed the ego and more than made up for the absence of a live audience when we recorded the programme in the studio. This was our stage, and upon it we all showed off outrageously and had lots and lots of fun.

One of the most exciting things about these appearances was that we never quite knew what was going to happen when we got to the appointed venue. There was one occasion that I will never forget, although today it is still hard to believe what happened. It was in 1953, just before the Coronation, and six of us went to be the celebrity guests at a Conservative rally. There were Dan and Doris, Mrs P and Walter Gabriel, Jack and Squire Fairbrother. We knew it was to be quite a special affair and had been told that the local mayor would give us lunch and that in the evening we would be guests for dinner of an earl. I do not know if that influenced Harry and the other men in their choice of dress, but certainly Pauline Seville (who plays Mrs P) and I took special care to look smart in honour of such exalted hosts. I wore one of my nicest 'fête-opening' dresses—black and white with tiny pleated panels that made me look slimmer—and I topped it off with a little black hat, long leather gloves and black shoes. The gloves and shoes were new for the occasion. Pauline, who is much younger and more sophisticated than her radio voice would let you believe, looked very elegant in a lovely silver-grey grosgrain dress.

Our troubles started during the morning, just before we were due at the mayor's parlour in the town hall. With unerring precision, a passing pigeon blessed Pauline with a horrible dropping on the back of her dress. Trying to be helpful, I rushed her into the ladies' loo and tried to wipe it off with paper hankies. Of course, I only succeeded in making an awful mess, and poor Mrs P spent a pre-lunch cocktail party trying to keep her back to the wall.

Just before the mayoral lunch, we were taken to have a quick look at the town's pride and joy—a new open-air swimming-pool. I cannot for the life of me think why, but I was invited to see the view from the top of the diving platform. As I clambered up, I remembered thinking that all the water on the hand-rail would not do my new gloves any good. It didn't—and neither did it do a lot for my new shoes. When I sat down for lunch and peeled off my gloves, I had navy-blue hands. And then when I crossed my ankles, they turned navy blue as well! Between us, Pauline and I must have been a sorry sight, but there was worse to come.

At the afternoon rally, there was a procession around the arena. Dan and I were in a Land-Rover at the front, with Walter and Mrs P in a pony and trap behind, and Jack and Mr Fairbrother on a brand-new tractor behind them. The noise of the tractor starting up startled the pony. But the person driving our Land-Rover had been told to keep at the head all the time, so when the pony bolted, we drove round and round at a terrific speed and Dan and I fell flat on the floor with our feet waving in the air. They had taken great care in cleaning the outside of the Land-Rover, but they had obviously not been expecting Dan and Doris Archer to be rolling around on the floor, which was pretty dirty. Can you imagine what I must have looked like when I eventually arrived at the earl's stately home? But ever forward, I asked if I might have a bath before dinner. Neither his lordship nor his staff batted an eyelid at such a request, and I was immediately shown to the bathroom. Once in the bath, I luxuriated for much longer than I had intended and by the time I got back downstairs looking all pink and glowing, all the others were glowing too—from all the drinks they had had to take while waiting for me! Everyone, I'm sure, heaved a great sigh of relief—our hosts when we had gone and us when we finally got home.

Factories were not often on our schedules—we were agricultural folk after all—but I had a special interest in one that we were invited to visit in Northamptonshire. It was a shoe factory and during the tour I was able to tell the machinists all about how the leather used to be cut by hand and how it was then moulded round the last. I was delighted to overhear one of the men say: 'That Doris Archer isn't half clever. D'you reckon she had a briefing like they gave the King when he came here?' I did not tell him that my 'briefing' had come from years watching my father and his men in the shop back in Wolverhampton. Harry Oakes was also able to show off a bit: he knew that the scars on a piece of leather lying on a workbench had been caused by the animal rubbing itself on a wire fence. Between us, we earned the equivalent of a standing ovation. As we left, the workers broke into a half-chanted, half-hummed rendering of The Archers' signature tune. We were quite used to hearing 'Barwick Green' played on varying qualities of pianos and other musical instruments, but that is the only time I heard folk trying to sing it.

Not long after that, I went to open a garden fête in Stevenage. A pianist was there to provide the usual playing of music, but just as I made my entrance, she switched from the signature tune to 'Happy Birthday to You' and the entire audience burst into spontaneous song. Covered in confusion, I tried to back out, to let the birthday girl hold the centre stage, until one of the organizers said: 'But it's for you, Mrs Archer!' Then, in horror: 'It *is* your birthday, isn't it?' I was about to say it was, just to save the poor woman's embarrassment, when she added: 'I'm sure I heard Dan saying last night that he had a surprise arranged for your birthday today.' She was right, it *was* Doris's birthday.

That little incident brought home to me that many of the listeners knew Doris Archer better than I did. You see, they heard everything about her, all the bits of background information and gossip from all the other characters in the programme. I was only aware of the stuff that came out of scenes I was actually in. All that, of course, deepened the confusion over the differences between the actors and their radio characters. At a very posh 'do' given by the National Farmers' Union, Harry Oakes and I were chatting when a fairly well-known stockbreeder came up and bottonholed Harry: 'Come and have a drink, Dan. I've got a beautiful bunch of heifers coming on. Just what

86

you need at your place.' Harry, who seldom lost the opportunity to be wicked, grinned and asked: 'Do you think they'd feed all right in my little suburban garden?' The poor stockbreeder was nonplussed: 'Good heavens, you don't mean to say you're not a farmer!' John Franklyn, the actor who played Mike Daly, a rather mysterious Irishman, was one day standing in a bus queue talking to his wife, and a woman obviously overheard him and recognized his voice: 'You are Mike Daly in The Archers, aren't you? Oh I am pleased to meet you. All my family said you were fiction, but I knew you must be real!'

Sometimes not being what I seemed had its awkward moments, but more often it was highly amusing. As Doris Archer, farmer's wife, I was always around the cowsheds, happily feeding the animals and pushing them around where I needed them to be. As Gwen Berryman, actress, I was scared stiff of cows and I hated it whenever they were around and I had to pose with them for photographs during visits to agricultural shows. On the other hand, I did see the funny side of the different marital status of Doris and Gwen. I soon got used to all the witticisms about being 'the most famous unmarried mother' in the country. I was a bit worried on one occasion, however, when a lady who had heard me described as Miss Berryman was quite outraged: 'You and that Archer man should be ashamed of yourselves. You jolly well ought to get married, even if it's just for the sake of your grand-children!'

My father found that kind of remark much more upsetting than I did and one day, after hearing it in front of some of our friends, he went off and bought me a ring. It was an enormous jade setting and when I wore it on the third finger of my left hand, you could not see whether there was a wedding ring there or not.

There was another problem about playing Doris Archer that a lot of folk could not understand. Whenever there was a particularly intriguing story going on in the programme, everyone always wanted to know the outcome in advance. They would not believe me when I said that I could not tell them even if I wanted to. They could not understand that I had nothing to do with the writing of the programme. There was often downright disbelief in their faces: 'You're not trying to say no one consults you about what they're going to expect you to do next?' To the ordinary listener, it was difficult to accept that we—whom they saw as the stars and therefore the most important people—had no involvement in the production. Certainly they attributed all the happenings to us; for example, I got the blame when a woman's cat got caught in a gin-trap that had evidently been set by someone who heard about that kind of device on The Archers. Although in fact we had the perfectly normal—and quite proper—relationship with the writers and producer, our constant exposure to the public did sometimes make us feel like pawns on Godfrey Baseley's chessboard. I think our 'stardom' gave us an inflated idea of our own importance and on the one occasion we abandoned our 'merely-actors role' and asked for some say in the development of the story, we were very quickly shot down in flames. On sober reflection, I for one knew that we had been wrong even to think about it. We had quite enough on our plates as actors, continually striving for better performances—which is, after all, what the public really want of our profession.

CHAPTER FIVE

I discovered early on that one of the penalties of being constantly in the public eye is that you virtually become public property. Certainly, the press seemed to have a voracious appetite for snippets of personal information. Usually it was quite flattering to be asked for an interview and by far the vast majority of the many journalists I met were very nice people, well disposed to The Archers. They were always genuinely interested in getting the kind of story that added colour to the general picture and I have hundreds of newspaper clippings illustrating how reliable these men and women were. I have also got a couple of not-so-nice items written by journalists who were either very careless in taking down shorthand, or who were deliberately vicious.

There was one man in particular who really made my blood boil when I read his article in a national weekly paper. He was pleasant enough when he came to see me and he seemed to be a genuine fan of The Archers, because he knew all about the programme and what had been going on during the previous few weeks. From gossip about the goings-on in Ambridge, the conversation moved on to a more personal level with comparisons being made between me and Doris Archer: I was a middle-aged urban spinster, who liked to wear nice clothes, could not stand housework but quite enjoyed cooking and baking; she was slightly older, a countrywoman, farmer's wife and grandmother, and was reputed to keep her farmhouse very neat and tidy. So, yes, I conceded we were quite different personalities; and yes, I agreed, I had said we were not really compatible as friends. We moved on, leaving Doris Archer behind. What were my hobbies? I dabbled in lots of things with little spectacular success: my golf was poor; my ice-skating fair; my gardening, enthusiastic; and my holiday cruising my favourite pastime. We moved on again, but now

I noticed a slight embarrassment. Would I mind awfully if he asked one or two questions about marriage and men? Not in the slightest, why should I? I was only a spinster because of a series of unfortunate circumstances, and I had never made any secret of the fact that I would have preferred to marry. Then came the real source of embarrassment: what did I think of my current prospects? I just burst out laughing, partly because of the young man's blushing (this was still in the early fifties, remember) but also because I had never really weighed up my 'prospects'. Then I made a joke about not being able to find anyone of my age who looked like Errol Flynn! But more seriously, I went on to explain that my mother had died a year or so earlier and that my father had had a stroke, leaving him in need of constant attention. I could not even think about anything else while he was still ill, I said.

When the newspaper was published the next weekend, I could hardly believe what I read. I was absolutely shattered, not just by the sensationally-big headline: 'Britain's most famous unmarried mum waits for her Errol Flynn', not even by the first paragraph that described me as 'plump and pleasant' and said I still 'thought constantly of matrimony'. It was the final sentence which upset me so much: 'She'll have a look round when her father's gone.'

From what I have written earlier in this book, it will be obvious to everyone how much my father meant to me and just how strong an influence he had been in my career and in my life. With him at home so ill and still full of grief after my mother's death, I could not take the sheer callousness of the remark and I burst into tears. The very idea that I should be sitting there waiting for my father to die so that I could go off in search of a husband was grotesque. It made me sound very heartless. I was glad, in a way, that my father was actually too poorly to read the paper. I dread to think what his reaction would have been if he had seen it.

Luckily it was not a paper read by too many of my friends and relatives, so there was no distressing reaction from that quarter. I did, however, get letters from one or two Archers listeners saying how sorry they were that I thought so little of my father that I was only concerned about my own future, and that I therefore was not fit to play a decent woman like Doris Archer. Some others said how disgusting it was to read about a woman of my age chasing after men.

I wrote an angry letter to the editor of the newspaper and I sent a copy of it to all the people who wrote to me. I am not sure if it did any good in either case: the newspaper did not bother to apologize and I never heard again from any of the offended fans.

The other instance I had of being totally misunderstood was not in anything I said to the newspapers but in what I did *not* say on the wireless. I was a keen member of the Soroptimist Club, and on one occasion I agreed to make an appeal for money—in *The Week's Good Cause*—to help run the Club's old people's home in Wolverhampton. During the appeal I was trying to show that we were not just asking other people to help and I said: 'We ourselves are working like—well I won't say *what* we're working like—to raise funds.' It was then the BBC received what was labelled its craziest-ever complaint: a caller rang to say that I had insulted coloured people. I was flabbergasted. What I had been going to say was 'working like hell', but then I remembered that I was Doris Archer and that it was Sunday, so I decided at the last minute to change it to 'working like the very devil', and I even thought better of that before going into the studio, so in the end avoided saying anything at all. There was certainly nothing in my mind about coloured people and I would not dream of insulting them. The well-known BBC spokesman for once hit the right note in his comment to the press: 'It seemed an innocent remark. We really can't tell broadcasters to be careful about the things they do *not* say on the air.'

I remember a much happier story about something that *was* said in The Archers and the effect it had on a little girl in Daventry, Northamptonshire. The girl had, some years earlier, lost most of the sight in her right eye after it had been damaged in an accident with a pen. Her mother had taken her to the hospital in Northampton, where the doctors could do little to help but suggested she attended clinics every twelve months. After five years without result, the mother began to despair. Then she heard The Archers one evening and suddenly she found new hope. In the programme, Philip Archer overturned his tractor on Lakey Hill and sustained injuries that threatened his sight. But after the usual cliff-hanging suspense, listeners heard that he was to undergo an operation in which his damaged lens was replaced with a new one. Aware of The Archers' reputation for accuracy, the woman began to wonder if the seemingly-miraculous operation was something more than a figment of Edward J. Mason's fertile imagination. When she took her daughter for her latest annual check-up, she made inquiries and found out that it definitely was possible, and in fact another patient at that hospital was then being prepared for it. The mother was delighted and told the local paper that listening to the The Archers had given her new hope: 'There must be thousands who drew hope as I did from Philip Archer's good fortune and I'm certainly grateful to the programme.'

It was nice to know that we could offer that

sort of comfort to people. I wish I could report that the mother's hopes were fulfilled and the little girl had the operation to restore her sight. Sadly, when I made inquiries recently, I found that it did not work out that way and neither the hospital nor the girl—now, of course, a woman in her forties—could tell me why. The operation was accurately described in the programme and it could have been available to the girl, but as it was not done, she is still blind in one eye.

CHAPTER SIX

Lots of people over the years have tried to explain the amazing success of The Archers and, particularly at this late stage in events, I cannot see much mileage in joining in the analysis game. But having already acknowledged Godfrey Baseley's key role in getting the whole project started, I want to pay tribute to Tony Shryane who I think played the vital part in keeping it so safely on the rails. Right from the beginning there was a punishing schedule for recordings and it was Tony's meticulous planning that made it work. But, more important, he always exercised his obvious authority with a quiet charm that endeared him to the actors and actresses. Any temperament he might have had was well hidden from us, and nerves and neuroses seemed to be a privilege only allowed to artistes. Where Godfrey kept us on tenterhooks, Tony was more likely to cosset us.

An example of his ability to care equally about the programme and the people who worked on it occurred when, some time in our second year, I went down with bronchitis and just could not get out of bed to go to the studio. I was very unhappy and felt that I was letting everyone down. Tony knew that and, rather than have me written out of the scripts for a while, he suggested that we record one or two scenes in my house. I thought he was joking—until Harry Oakes and Tony arrived, accompanied by two engineers carrying microphone, cable and all the other paraphernalia of broadcasting. I did not even stir from my bed: they converted my room into a studio and, just as we would have back in the proper studio, Harry and I immediately became Dan and Doris. I wonder what a certain journalist might have written had he known just how realistic were the subsequent bedroom scenes between the man with two wives and the most famous unmarried mother in Britain.

But that kind of caring and consideration was typical of Tony. When, in 1954, Robert Mawdesley died and Chris Gittins was brought in to take over the role of Walter Gabriel, it was Tony who shrugged off all public criticism of the change and persuaded his masters to give

Chris time to settle in.

It was in the same year that the efforts of Tony and the rest of us were rewarded. The Archers shared first place with *Take It From Here* in the National Radio Awards sponsored by the *Daily Mail*. I do not know why—we had lots of evidence of success—but we were all surprised by the award. I am not sure if there were nominations or anything like that. If there were, we did not hear about it until suddenly we had won and we all got very excited. I think sharing the award with another programme like Jimmy Edwards' *Take It From Here* actually enhanced it for us. That was a very successful radio show and to be so favourably compared with it gave us a new context in which to view The Archers. Although the long run—we had been going for three years by then—made it obvious that we had audience-appeal, I do not think I had thought in terms of being in an important national radio show. Perhaps it was because we worked in Birmingham that we did not quite realize the scale of our achievement. The award helped to change all that and when we went to the presentation evening at the Scala Theatre, I felt we were taking our rightful place alongside some of the great names of broadcasting—Gilbert Harding, Franklin Engelmann and Richard Dimbleby, who were all there in various capacities. It was a great occasion, marred slightly for me by the fact that

I turned out to be wearing an almost identical dress to that of Lady Jacob, wife of Sir Ian Jacob, then Director-General of the BBC. Luckily she, too, had a sense of humour and we were both able to laugh it off.

I met Sir Ian again later in the year when he hosted a party to celebrate The Archers' one-thousandth episode and presented each of us with a lovely silver cigarette-box inscribed with our initials. Harry Oakes said the 'GB' on my box meant 'Great Berryman' and, as it happened to be my forty-eighth birthday, I had an extra glass of champagne. Those, of course, were the good old days, when the BBC was still able to live quite well off the licence fee.

1954 was obviously quite a hectic year and I see from my diary I went to London on two separate occasions for the one event—to take part in the very popular television panel game *What's My Line?*, which was hosted by Eamonn Andrews and featured, among others, Lady Isobel Barnett. I was furious about the first occasion because after having gone all the way to London with Harry Oakes and two or three other members of the cast, and having sat around for several hours, we were eventually told that because of a mix-up we would not be able to take part after all. I was really very cross because the trouble was created by Godfrey Baseley again raising his argument about us not being seen so as not to destroy the listeners' illusions. As almost everyone in the cast had already been pictured in almost every newspaper in the country, I could not see that there were many illusions left. And in any case, all that should have been resolved before the invitation was ever extended to us. Eventually, as happened over the newspaper pictures a couple of years earlier, Godfrey either changed his mind or was over-ruled, and some time later Harry Oakes and I did appear as celebrity guests on *What's My Line?* and the panel guessed who we were almost at once. Another little pointer, I thought, to our popularity.

Our popularity as celebrities on the great garden fête circuit also caused a row that year. We used to receive hundreds of invitations every summer and I can honestly say we did not do very much picking and choosing about which we would attend. We usually operated a first-come, first-served principle. What neither the cast nor the BBC noticed was that we opened quite a few Tory fêtes but very few for the Labour Party. That, of course, was entirely due to the social structures of the two parties: the Tories simply held many more of that kind of function. That, however, did not stop a Labour MP complaining that when Dan and Doris were seen to open a Conservative fête in East Anglia, The Archers—and therefore the BBC—was seen to show political favour to the right. So, Harry and I had to go the fêtes under our real names, which did not mean half as much to people as Dan and Doris Archer. The BBC told us we must not use our character names nor give any indication of our association with The Archers when we attended political functions. We never did open any more Tory—or Labour or Liberal—fêtes after that, although personally I thought it was all very silly and petty.

The next year in The Archers was very much the year-of-Grace. After a long, on-off-on relationship, Philip Archer and Grace Fairbrother finally declared their intention to have an Easter wedding and that brought in shoals of letters from all over Britain. As the bridegroom's mother, most of my correspondents wanted me to stop Philip making a terrible mistake because Grace was not the right girl for him. Leslie Bowmar, who played her father, got letters saying the opposite. But Norman Painting and Ysanne Churchman, the happy couple, had lots of good wishes from hundreds of enthusiastic listeners.

When the wedding day finally dawned, Tony Shryane arranged for a mock service to be recorded at what we now regarded as our own parish church, at Hanbury. When we got there for the recording, we were staggered to find an enormous crowd milling around outside, with the village bobby desperately trying to control them. I do not know how the people found out we were going to be there, but it seemed as if no one wanted to miss Grace's wedding—although her father and the best man nearly did! Leslie Bowmar and Denis Folwell (Jack) could not park anywhere near the church and then, after walking the last mile, had great difficulty in getting into the church. And we were almost prevented from recording the service after all that. The parson had to make an announcement from the pulpit asking for some drivers to move their vehicles to let the BBC recording-car through.

My strongest memories of the occasion were the awful noise in the church—with everyone chattering away so that I could not even hear what was being said—and the noise made later by one of the church newspapers, which thought the 'ceremony' should not have been allowed to take place in a real church. The critics, and I can see their point, were offended by the use of the church as a kind of theatre. One of the more irreverent wags in the cast said they were just jealous 'because we got a better house than they've managed for years'. Luckily, the local rector did not hear that remark (though on reflection he had a good sense of humour and would have laughed with the rest of us) and our relations with him remained very good. We were allowed to go on making recordings there and to use the church as a back-cloth for many of our publicity photographs.

The wedded bliss of Grace and Philip was, of

course, to be short-lived. But before that make-believe tragedy stunned listeners, I had a personal tragedy that left me with little thought about anything else. My father died.

It is difficult to explain just how important Dad had been to me without making it sound over-sentimental, but he really was an amazing, romantic character with a powerful personality and I know just how much he shaped my own personality. He gave me my passion for music, he gave me the desire to perform and he gave me the determination to be successful. I was enthralled by the stories of his childhood and the Victorian poverty of his upbringing. I am still starry-eyed in my admiration at the way he was able so to 'improve' himself that he not only overcame his bad start in life but conducted his later years with so much style. No one who knew him in business would ever have guessed at his early background although, of course, he never tried to cover it up or pretend to be anything he was not.

He and my mother were what other people might describe as doting parents. I, of course, really just saw them as Mum and Dad and took them for granted most of the time. I think I probably did not appreciate the sacrifices they must have made to put me through my music lessons and my training at the Royal Academy of Music. I also assumed that all parents were so interested in their children's activities that they would just sit for hours listening to me prattle on and on about what I had been doing, who I had met and what they had said. (Readers can thank—or blame—my parents for this book: it was their encouragement to share my experiences with them that has left me the ability to recall all sorts of little details about my life.) More than that, they always made sure that I was well dressed and though Mum may sometimes have overdone the ribbons and bonnets, I appreciated nice clothes from a very early stage. They also endowed me with the confidence to wear the clothes with some style, by making the photographer's studio almost like an extension of our home. Every birthday, without fail—and at every other opportunity—I was put in front of a camera and encouraged to pose until it became second nature to me to hold myself well.

When my mother died suddenly in 1952, the sharpness was taken out of the blow by the need to comfort Dad. When he died there was no such responsibility, nothing to protect me from the savage feelings of despair at my loss. I can only say I wallowed in self-pity and grief. It was time and the unrelenting demands of The Archers that took me out of myself and allowed me to realize that life must go on.

But, of course, as my life went on, it almost immediately brought me back to death—that of Grace, after only a few months of marriage to

Philip Archer. It was this incident in the programme more than anything else that highlighted the degree of confusion between reality and fantasy in the minds of listeners.

The reaction to Grace's death was amazing, with thousands of messages of sympathy pouring into the BBC and people even sending flowers and wreaths. I thought it odd that people could be aware enough to address things to the BBC offices, but bewildered enough to believe that there actually had been a death. Mind you, I have to confess that I was pretty shaken by the incident myself. I was not in that episode and when I heard it on the air, I could hardly believe my ears and I cried every bit as much as I might have done over a real daughter-in-law. One of my more cynical friends, however, suggested that my distress was less for poor, dear Grace and more because of the fact that her demise simply underlined the vulnerability of the artiste to the whim of the writers. I can assure you that insecurity is so deep in the soul of most performers that no one needs to be reminded of the precariousness of their position.

Even in a long-running programme like The Archers, we never felt very safe. In fact, Godfrey Baseley often made a point of reminding us how he had us in the palm of his hand and had complete control of our immediate future. If he was just trying to keep us all on our toes, then I think he failed. All that happened was that most of us just became more neurotic than ever.

My own peace of mind was hardly helped with the awful realization that, having been away from the theatre for so long, there was little hope of getting back on stage. When I accepted the first contract for The Archers it was just another job in broadcasting, interesting and well paid though it was. I did not see it as an alternative to the stage but more as a complement, enabling me to widen my experience. Even after nearly five years, I thought I could simply trot along to the nearest repertory theatre, remind them of my long years of experience, give them the good news that I was no longer tied exclusively to the wireless and then wait to be told what starring roles would be mine. It was when I ventured along that road that I learned, at first hand, the problems of typecasting.

I was not exactly fed up with The Archers, but especially during my father's long illness, I had found the constant commitment quite a strain and I thought that it would be nice to have a break and go back to the thrill of the live theatre. I still had lots of friends and good contacts in several repertory companies, so I started dropping hints that I could be available for the right parts. Nohing happened. I started dropping hints that I might be available, full stop. Nothing happened. In the end I said I was available and would be happy to consider any good meaty parts. It was a friend who explained the problem: I was typecast in my role as Doris Archer. 'Your voice is much too well known for me to be able to cast you in one of our productions,' my friend told me. 'The audience wouldn't be watching the play, they'd be listening to Doris Archer, who they would see as pretending to be an actress, who in turn was pretending to be a character in the play. Can you imagine how confusing that could be?'

I could. I knew I would have to go on being Doris Archer. I did not see it at the time, but that fictional farmer's wife was developing a life of her own, and it was intruding more and more into mine.

CHAPTER SEVEN

Being called Doris a lot more often than I was called Gwen was bound to have some effect. Even many of my friends used the character name, so it was inevitable that I automatically responded to the 'Hello, Doris' greetings in my radio voice, and that obviously suggests that I was subconsciously accepting that I was Doris Archer. Now I, like everyone else in the country, knew Doris Archer was a countrywoman with a husband, three children and three grandchildren, so I must, deep down, have started to feel that's what I was.

Such confusion was compounded by the fact that the scriptwriters had by now recognized all my natural speech patterns and vocal idiosyncrasies, so that they were producing dialogue that sounded just like Gwen Berryman. They had also picked up a fair bit about my own personal interests and so Doris began to use my voice to talk about cooking, gardening, needlework and so on, exactly the way I did myself.

I would probably have been able to avoid too much of a merger if I could have left Doris behind in the studio, but the success of The Archers precluded any possibility of that. The constant demands for personal appearances were such that I had to take my radio persona with me wherever I went. Quite simply, the public were not much interested in meeting a middle-aged actress called Gwen Berryman and so, to gain attention—which, I readily confess, I absolutely loved—I *was* Doris Archer at garden fêtes and other functions right across the country.

I do not think I was changing my own personality very much. I did not become the farmer's wife in any particular way. I mean, I never wore tweeds or gumboots or anything like that. I loved clothes and I always took great care over the way I looked. My bank manager can tell you about the fortune I have spent on dresses and hats! I did have a quite extravagant life-style, collecting lovely antiques and exquisite lace, and always driving fairly flashy cars. What must have been happening, I think, was an enlarging of my personality to encompass Doris Archer.

Most of the time, I would have said she was in a kind of watertight compartment. But every now and again there must have been some leakage. I noticed it first when I started feeling resentful of Dorothy Oakes being introduced, as she often was, as Mrs Archer. As I have already made clear, Harry and Dorothy were both very good friends of mine and I never minded Harry's quips about his two wives. But every now and again I found myself getting quite cross when someone at one of our public appearances got mixed up and introduced them as Dan and Doris. It is not easy to explain, because I never saw Harry as my husband, but he was my Dan—if that makes any kind of sense?

I worried for a time that I was actually resenting Dorothy for stealing some of my limelight, that I was becoming scared of losing my audience. One of the penalties of being treated like a star is that it can allow you to indulge in fits of temperament and to make unreasonable demands on the people around you. It also exposes any flaws in your

108

personality and I thought I might be seeing a horrible crack—jealousy—opening up in mine. Perhaps I was, but I feel better about putting it all down to the phenomenon of a two-in-one personality.

I think it was because I was aware of the dangers in allowing my career to become an obsession that I always tried to maintain a separate existence away from The Archers, although not always successfully. I was, for example, a very active member of the Soroptimist Club and when I was offered the chance of going to the international convention in New York in 1956, I accepted and took time off from the programme to join four other delegates from Wolverhampton on the transatlantic trip. I do not suppose I was very popular in The Archers' office because it again meant that I had to be written out of the script, but it was a lovely break, which I think probably did the programme as much good as it did me.

We sailed from Liverpool and had a very leisurely journey to New York, but once in America it was a different story—I was rushed off my feet. Apart from trying to see all the sights and doing some shopping, I was given the job of organizing some traditional entertainment on behalf of the British Federation of Clubs. I had known about it before we left and I had some ideas up my sleeve, but I could not actually get on with it until I met all our

Federation's delegates and assessed the talent. There was plenty of it, and between us we put on a really sparkling show in the very grand dining-room of the plush Waldorf-Astoria. I remember it had a very patriotic ending—a tableau in which we showed how the Union Jack was made from the separate crosses of St George, St Patrick and St Andrew—and as that was happening I read a script specially written for the occasion by Norman Painting. It was a great success. We were given a standing ovation from the thousand or so guests and I had to wait for nearly five minutes—loving every second of it, of course—while the applause continued, before I could speak the closing words. It was the kind of response you can only get from a live audience and it was a real tonic to a professional.

Some British tourist trade people were in the audience and they later told the press that our show—and especially the flag sequence—had done more for Britain's prestige in New York than anything had for many years. I was very pleased to hear that comment because one of the things that surprised me most about the Americans was that they all thought England was almost permanently under a pall of fog or swept by heavy rain. They had got that picture from a television series about Sherlock Holmes, in which the great detective always seemed to be looking for clues in foggy London or on the rain-lashed moors of Yorkshire.

Another thing that surprised me was that I was well enough known there to be invited to appear on radio and television. I did go on two radio programmes but when faced with the choice of appearing on television or having an afternoon by the sea, I plumped for the latter. In fact, I had been having trouble with my feet— because of New York's heat and hard pavements—and I spent most of that day soaking my feet in the briny down at Long Island. The salt gave me temporary relief, but by the time I got back to England—on the *Queen Elizabeth*—they were all swollen again, a fact that did not go unnoticed by the sharp-eyed gentlemen of Fleet Street. One of the popular papers reported: 'Gwen Berryman, better known as homely Doris Archer of the you-know-which radio serial, shuffled down the gangway of the *Queen Elizabeth* yesterday—in shoes two sizes too big.' Undignified as my return might have been, it was good to be back in Britain and a relief to get back into Doris Archer's shoes. They were certainly more comfortable than my own.

Almost at once I slipped back into the routine. After disembarking at Southampton, I went straight to Morecambe to join Harry Oakes and, as Dan and Doris, we switched on the local illuminations. Then, after a day or so catching up with my sleep, it was back to the studio for recording sessions and to pick up my mail.

Doris had her birthday while I was away, and all her cards, and some presents, were waiting for me. I felt a bit like the Queen, with two birthdays.

Those presents, which came on birthdays and at Christmas, were quite an embarrassment sometimes. I did not mind when people sent small gifts like handkerchiefs—I have still got quite a few with the letter 'D' embroidered in the corner—or even scarves and chair-back covers, but I got worried by some of the more expensive items that arrived because you could nearly always tell that the sender could not really afford the gift. I was always desperately anxious not to offend anyone, but at the same time I could not let hard-working folk waste their money on me. Diplomatic letters usually did the trick, although I suspect one or two illusions were shattered when Doris Archer fans got polite notes from somebody called Gwen Berryman.

I could never quite fathom why people sent gifts. What, I wonder, was in their mind when they went to buy—or even make—a present, wrap it up and then post it? Who did *they* think they were sending it to as they wrote 'Mrs Doris Archer' and almost always, 'c/o the BBC' either in London or in Birmingham? Assume for a moment that it was intended for Doris Archer: that means they would have believed that she was a real farmer's wife living in a place called

Ambridge. So why address it to the BBC and not to the village? Then take it the other way round: they realized that Doris was not real but wanted to send something to me. So why not address it to Gwen Berryman?

It was the fiction of Doris crossed with the fact of the BBC that puzzles me still. Perhaps the answer is that they were only half confused at the time—which means they were probably half a step ahead of me!

CHAPTER EIGHT

The newspapers and magazines never seemed to tire of writing about The Archers but, as the years rolled by, it must have become increasingly difficult for the writers to find something new to say about us. Each member of the cast had been interviewed dozens of times and you would see the same little incidents and the *bon mots* reported in paper after paper. I have got an extensive collection of newspaper cuttings and in nearly of them I'm scared of cows, friendly and approachable, an excellent cook, and either just what one would expect or not a bit like what one imagined.

In 1957, to try to get away from the norm, one women's magazine, instead of interviewing me, took me to a well-known clairvoyant and asked him what he saw in the crystal for me. At least he was not confused about whose future he was reading. 'I've got some good news for you, Gwen,' he said. 'Your programme will soon be on our television screens.' I was not all that sure that it *was* good news for me, but it sounded quite a fair prediction. Since the second channel had started a couple of years earlier, television was rapidly increasing in influence and its audience was growing at the expense of radio. Many of the people who switched from listening to watching must, of course, have been Archers' fans and there is no doubt in my mind that transferring the programme to the 'box' would have been quite a popular move. It had been suggested inside the BBC and, although I never knew any of the details, I gather the possibility was examined very carefully, and rejected.

The clairvoyant's other predictions had come in the form of gloomy warnings: I must take care of my health during the winter, 'especially when snow is on the ground,' and I must take care of my jewellery, too, 'as there is a possibility of a visit from a burglar.'

I must have heeded his warnings very well because, although there was quite a bit of snow that year, I escaped most of my usual bronchial ills; and my new kitten, Pixie (a present from a listener), succeeded in frightening off any would-be burglars. I went into 1958 with wealth and health as intact as could be expected.

If the clairvoyant's crystal had been less cloudy, he could have predicted: 'A good year ahead . . . even more hectic than usual . . . another ambition will be fulfilled . . . your lucky number is two thousand.'

The year started fairly quietly with only a passing reference to our seventh anniversary and all but one of the newspapers resisting the temptation to warn us of the dangers of a seven-year itch. The paper that yielded to temptation, one of the quality Sundays, noted the growing television audiences and said the 'box' was a kind of 'siren luring people to its mindlessness' and that The Archers, sadly, was 'one of the ships most likely to run aground'—another prediction that was not, as we now know, altogether accurate.

Not long afterwards, we had a visit from one of the Sundays at the other end of the market, and still conscious of the way I had been treated years earlier by a similar kind of newspaper, I kept what would today be described as a low profile. I did little more than shake hands and say hello to the reporter and photographer. But that, it seems, was enough—though this time there was nothing vicious in the article when it appeared the following Sunday. It was just that they got a lot more out of my greeting than I put into it. For example, my simple politeness was translated like this:

'Meet the most famous unmarried mother in the country!' boomed Jack across the bar, and I was shaking hands with the roly-poly, motherly figure who plays Doris Archer—Miss Gwen Berryman—who acknowledged her station in life with an infectious chuckle.

'I was introduced that way at a bazaar I was opening,' she told me, 'and it has stuck to me ever since. Mind? Why should I? I introduce myself that way now—and it always gets gales of laughter. Except once! There was one village hall which remained absolutely silent when I did my little piece. Not a titter! I couldn't understand it—I thought I must be slipping. Afterwards I had a quiet word with the vicar who took me gently by the arm and said: "What you did not understand, my dear, was that eighty per cent of this village is illegitimate!"'

The first part of the story was true and I suppose he got that from earlier cuttings about the programme, but where on earth he got the sting to put in the tail, I have no idea. Certainly not from me, and there was no truth in it either. But then, I think the young man was more interested in entertaining his readers than in informing them and he went on to attribute another quote to me.

'At one fête I was opening an old lady was wheeled up to me in a bath chair,' Gwen

116

Berryman told me. 'I'd done my piece about being the most famous, etcetera and the old lady hissed at me, "I'm disgusted! Disgusted that any woman could stand up in public and say such a thing, especially when you're married to Dan. I've heard you going to bed with him!"'

'She'd heard me say, "Move over!" to Doris,' laughed Dan. 'I explained to the old lady that where she hears the bed spring creak, there's a small boy with a large spring in the background twanging away. She would not believe me!'

That story has appeared in dozens of newspapers over the years and I still don't know who originated it! I had to chuckle at the way this particular article ended: 'They're real all right! Actors they may be but they love the characters they have created with such success as much as we do, and which is why I can still switch on at 6.45 at night—with my illusions intact.'

I wish *I* could say the same about my illusions about a certain newspaper. I really am glad I stuck to my simple 'Hello'. What would the reporter have been able to do with 'Nice to meet you' or some such revelation?

This extra flurry of press interest in The Archers was quite often the prelude to one of our numerous milestones and on this occasion it was the lead up to the two thousandth episode. Once again I found a picture of Dan and Doris on the front page of the *Radio Times*, and that to a broadcaster then was a bit like a model making the cover of *Vogue*. In a way, the acknowledgement of our peers in the specialist magazine was more important than the ordinary press coverage.

The BBC also marked the occasion with the publication of a newspaper called the *Borchester Echo* which, in the programme, was the weekly paper covering the Ambridge area. It was a brilliant promotional idea and it sold something like a million copies. It was also a classic example of our schizophrenia, containing a bewildering mixture of fact and fantasy. For example, I appeared for once as Gwen Berryman and wrote a short piece about what it was like to be two people at once:

Someone once said that life begins at forty. Well, certainly for me a new life began just after that age; for that was when I, a middle-aged spinster, was asked to become Doris, or Mrs Dan Archer. At first I thought this was going to be just another job, but I hadn't bargained for the fact that the Archers were to become universal favourites, a family whose ups and downs were to mean so much to so many.

I then went on to talk about the difficulty of trying to keep Gwen and Doris in separate compartments and added:

The reason was that the Archer family really became my family. For reasons I find it hard to explain, I became very fond of my husband and children. Yes, genuinely. Fond, too, of all the characters in the programme. This extension of my normal existence has made me feel that my life is richer for this experience. I remember once, when Dan had said that he did not like kippers for breakfast, a retired farm worker of over seventy wrote to tell me how to cook kippers to make them taste like boiled ham! He said he was sure Dan would enjoy them cooked that way. I didn't dare to write and tell the dear old soul that I had never actually cooked a meal for Harry (Dan) in my life. It might have spoiled the programme for him! Even now, after almost eight years, I think many people do not know where fiction ends in The Archers or truth begins. Indeed, I hardly know myself. After all, quite recently when Gwen Berryman had teething troubles, poor old Doris had to have teething troubles too, just in case new teeth for Gwen made Doris sound different!

While I was clearly labelled Gwen Berryman on this item, there was one on another page by 'Walter Gabriel' and there was a collection of pictures taken 'at Brookfield Farm'. No wonder we got confused.

One of the less sensitive features of the two-thousandth episode celebration was a roll call in the *Radio Times:*

Inevitably, in eight years, a few Ambridge folk have died. Bill Slater was the first to go, killed in a brawl. He was followed by Ben White (the baker), Grace Archer (Philip's first wife), Simon Cooper (Dan's farm-hand), Bob Larkin (a poacher) and the squire's wife. Others have gone with less finality, such as the hot-headed Irishman, Mike Daly, who rejoined the secret-service; Clive Lawson-Hope who chose to empire-build in Africa; and Elizabeth Lawson who failed to land the widowed Philip and returned to nursing.

I am sure it was not intended to remind those of us still around of our dramatic mortality but I can tell you it hardly made any of us feel any more secure!

In the wake of the two-thousandth episode, I realized an ambition—I had a book published. It was called *Doris Archer's Farm Cookery Book* but it contained quite a few of my own recipes, as well as some that had come to me from listeners. I was thrilled by the reception it got from the critics:

Of the making of cookery books there is seemingly no end, so I consider it to be a very large feather in Gwen Berryman's cap that she

120

has managed to create one which really does fill a gap.

I can truthfully say that I have never come across a publication which is as chockful as Miss Berryman's of invaluable, down-to-earth hints and recommendations. Moreover, this book is the genuine article, not just a string of recipes held together by one of the most famous and well loved names in radio.

Miss Berryman was reared in a tradition of good substantial food and has a real personal interest in the art of creating it. The atmosphere of good cooking with which the fictional character of Doris Archer has been surrounded is a true reflection of Miss Berryman's personal capabilities.

As might be expected, the recipes in this well filled book have a country air about them, with good homely fare and many farmhouse dishes. These should delight Archer fans and appeal to a host of housewives.

I was still basking in the success of the book when along came another chance to fulfil another ambition—to make a gramophone record. It was not exactly what I had originally had in mind when I was planning my great operatic and concert career, but a record was a record. Instead of my own selection of favourite arias, I was to be one of the cast on a special 45 rpm disc of The Archers.

To be honest, making the recording was not how I had imagined it, nor was it a bit like the films suggested. We just got together in the usual Birmingham studio and, perhaps a bit more nervously than normal, went through our party pieces. My contribution was to join Harry Oakes in a Dan-and-Doris duet, 'When We Are Married', and then, for what I think is called the flip side, we sat and reminisced about life in Ambridge.

There was more to the promotion of the record than there was to the making of it. The recording company was Pye and they arranged to launch The Archers (NEP 24096 on the Nixa label) at a reception in the Dorchester Hotel in London. Much to the entertainment of the well heeled guests of the Dorchester, we bowled up in a van bearing the legend: Borchester Bus, which purported to be a Walter Gabriel enterprise and was said to have brought us from the depth of rural England all the way to the bright lights. The truth is we had travelled about a mile in the van, from the BBC studios in Portland Place, W1. But the press, and that's who it was all laid on for, accepted the appearance of things rather than seeking any truths.

That also showed in some of the columns in the next morning's national newspapers. We were all depicted as a bunch of yokels, though I swear I was as smartly dressed as any of the hotel's patrons, and all the quotes were attributed to Dan, Doris and so on. I was reported to have had a *third* glass of champagne because it was my birthday. I did not and it wasn't. I had one glass and it was the day before my birthday—my own birthday, that is, not Doris's.

Mind you, I must not go on about the press, especially when our own people were adding to the confusion: a second edition of the *Borchester Echo* was published in 1959 and across the front page was the headline: 'Ambridge woman accused in gems case.' The illusion of it being the local paper covering Ambridge was continued with articles *about* Ned Larkin and Charles Grenville, and *by* Doris Archer, Walter Gabriel and John Tregorran. But then it was shattered by an item written by one of the senior BBC men and a digest of what had been happening in the story-line of the programme! With the BBC itself crossing and re-crossing the borderline so much, what hope did mere actors and actresses have of staying on the right side for any length of time?

I certainly tried, and I have a copy of an article I wrote for a women's magazine in 1959 in which I said: 'In the studio and on the air I feel, act and think exactly like Mrs Archer, but once outside the BBC I'm Gwen Berryman and as unlike Doris as it's possible to be.' I am pretty sure that is an honest reflection of the situation. However, in the same article I also wrote:

With over twelve million listeners following every instalment, I find that wherever I go there are people—from errand boys to earls—who know the Archer family almost as well as I do. This means that a lot of those people recognize me, and—although I know it is unusual in an actress—I loathe publicity. I hate women staring at me in shops, watching to see what I buy and how much I pay. I have never yearned for fame and I have never hankered after seeing my name in lights. I honestly do like acting for its own sake. I enjoy playing a character and entertaining audiences and during the war I worked in a repertory company for a small amount of money each week rather than give up the stage.

Now that was only partly true: I did hate the nosiness of some fans, but I loved everything else about being a star. I was probably suffering from confusion when I wrote the article!

But there's no doubt in my mind about what it was that left me more than ever bewildered about my double life—the illness of Harry Oakes, which began in the latter part of 1959. The difficulty began, I think, because of the way in which the writers decided to handle

Harry's absence when he had to be admitted to hospital. They sent Dan to hospital, too.

In the programme, Dan's problem was simple and uncomplicated—he had broken his leg—so Doris's hospital visits were similarly simple and uncomplicated: she was just the bearer of grapes and sympathy. Harry's real life situation was quite different. He had become the victim of a very punishing schedule of studio recordings followed by personal appearances followed by studio recordings. He was the pivot around which both the programme and its promotion revolved, so he must have worked harder than the rest of us, but, unlike me, he seldom took more than a fortnight's break at a time. Visits to his hospital bedside were not as straightforward as those the writers allowed Dan Archer. Harry was bright and cheerful and it was tempting to treat him as if his confinement were due to something as reparable as a broken leg. But the pallor of his face gave the lie to that: Harry was a very sick man, suffering from strain and complete nervous exhaustion. No one actually put it into words, but we were all very, very worried that he might not get well enough to go back to work.

The seriousness of Harry's illness and the simple injury to Dan were difficult to reconcile in my mind and, because it was obviously more comfortable, I think I let the fictional story have more credence. When Harry came out of hospital in time for Dan Archer to make an emotional Christmas reappearance at Brookfield Farm, the illusion was more or less complete: Harry Oakes, actor, had not really been very ill, he had just been playing the part of a farmer suffering the after-effects of a broken leg. Perhaps even Harry was taken in, because within weeks he was back in his old routine, working as hard as ever, cracking just as many jokes and charming just as many people with his twinkling smile.

Up until then there had never been any apparent thought about The Archers following the theatrical tradition of having understudies, but if the seriousness of Harry's health problems were underestimated by the cast, it was not by Godfrey Baseley and Tony Shryane. They decided that Dan Archer was so central to the programme that it would be harmful if he had to be written out from time to time. Sadly, Harry's physical condition deteriorated again, making that look more necessary, and after a lot of agonizing discussion, it was decided that Monte Crick should act as understudy to Harry. Monte had played one or two smaller parts in the programme and someone had noticed his voice was quite similar to the familiar tones of Harry.

As far as maintaining the continuity of the programme was concerned, Monte's appointment could not have been more timely. During the year, poor Harry Oakes became more and more ill. In a sometimes bitter interview in one of the national papers, he talked of the strain of being Dan Archer and listed the illnesses which had resulted from over-work: 'A heart attack, bronchitis, a nervous breakdown, a severe chill, stomach trouble, bronchitis (again), a throat-and-mouth infection and a third attack of bronchitis.' No wonder the paper used the headline: 'The astonishing burden of the nation's farmer-figure.'

It was, of course, his awareness of how important his role was to the success of The Archers that kept Harry going. Despite now having a stand-in, he tried desperately not to let his health interfere with the recordings. At first he let himself be helped up the two flights of stairs to the studio, then he had to be carried up, and finally, as they had done for me, Tony Shryane and his staff went to his home to record at his bedside.

The programme's tenth anniversary came in the middle of Harry's illness and he could not join in any of the celebrations. We all missed his presence very much. He, I suspect, would not have allowed a television team to give us a rough ride on what was supposed to be a happy occasion.

Prior to a party in the television studio in Birmingham—where a mock-up of The Bull had been arranged—some of us were invited on to the very popular *Tonight* programme, only to be asked questions obviously designed to make us look silly. Whether or not they succeeded I don't know, but they made me feel very cross. I think it was the last straw and I can't honestly say I saw too much to celebrate then, but being an actress, I just about managed to maintain some semblance of cheerfulness until I got home and cried!

When Harry died later in the year, I was very, very sad. I had seen him make himself ill and could do nothing to stop him or even make him slow down. The Archers had meant everything to him and he desperately did not want to let anyone down. And, of course, at the time he had meant so much to the programme that his death made me feel everything was beginning to fall apart.

Over the years, Harry had become a very good friend and a marvellous colleague to work with. Both of us had come from comparative obscurity and had shared all the excitement of success—an experience which, in itself, would have been enough to create a special bond. But, of course, on top of all that there was our man-and-wife relationship in the programme. If, as I have tried to show, that seemed a reality to our listeners, the fiction nevertheless gave us an incredible understanding of each other.

I was convinced that all this was a vital factor in the overall success of The Archers: to take away such an important ingredient would be to cause everything to fall flat. When I cried for Harry, I cried for much more besides.

CHAPTER NINE

There can have been few people who envied Monte Crick his new job. It is true that he had done very well when he had stepped into Harry's shoes as a temporary measure, but to move into the programme, in the leading role, on a permanent basis was a different proposition altogether. Not only had Harry created the character, but he had also endowed it with all his own style and personality; so much so that, to the public, he *was* Dan Archer—tall, broad-shouldered, grey-haired, thinning on top, neat grey moustache and a pair of twinkling, happy eyes. Monte did not look a bit like Harry, nor, therefore, like Dan Archer. He was younger for a start and not so tall. His hair was black and thick and his face was dominated by heavy, dark eyebrows and a moustache to match.

Nor was it just the problem of gaining acceptance from listeners that Monte had to face. He had to come into a close-knit little community where all the individuals had their own neuroses and complexes, and were too full of self-concern to be over-enthusiastic about newcomers. In other words, we were a clique.

I am sure no one tried to make things difficult for Monte—he was a lovely, friendly man—but at the same time, I am not sure that we could have been of any great help. We were all too upset to do much more than protect ourselves from the worst effects of having our vulnerability underlined and our insecurity heightened.

But, if he did not look much like my Dan Archer, Monte sounded unnervingly like him. He had, of course, worked hard to establish a believable similarity and the scriptwriters helped by using their skill to perpetuate Harry's speech patterns. I found it very disconcerting at first and it was quite some time before I stopped seeing Harry's face whenever I was listening to the new Dan's voice.

By the time I realized that Harry's death did not, after all, mean the end of the programme and my career, Monte had quietly settled in. I was full of admiration for the speed with which he achieved the transformation and very grateful, too, for the way he had managed it without ever once intruding into my relationship with Harry. He was a really good actor and a very nice man who did not spoil anything about the programme. He never once tried to assume the respect and affection that he could see so obviously had been Harry's. And, of course, in not trying, he gained both the more quickly.

My initial fear of him soon wore off as we became mutually-admiring colleagues and then good friends. Our friendship was enhanced by a common interest in music—Monte was an accomplished pianist, who had played professionally before becoming an actor.

I had particular cause to be grateful to Monte Crick for the smooth transition and the way he helped Dan and Doris to get back on an even keel, because in addition to the emotional stress, I was just beginning to have health problems as well. Ever since having a tubercular gland when I was a child, I had not exactly enjoyed the most robust health, with regular bouts of bronchial trouble if the wind was in the wrong direction and even a severe attack of pneumonia on one occasion. But this time it was nothing to do with my chest. It was the after-effects of an accident and the beginning of a painful affliction that was to be with me for the rest of my life.

About a year before Harry Oakes died, I was going down some stairs at Paddington Station when I fell head-long and ended up with a broken arm and bruises in all sorts of funny places. It was a terrifying experience and I was really very pleased that the young policeman who came to help me was an Archers fan and recognized my voice. He arranged for an ambulance to take me to hospital—where I found that even accidents can have their funny side. After all the X-rays and other investigations in the casualty department, it was decided that I should be admitted because of shock. As I was being wheeled into the ward on a rather noisy old stretcher trolley, one of the other women patients complained about the disturbance. 'Can't you keep quiet. I'm trying to listen to The Archers,' she said, very loudly and very rudely. I was both abashed and amused. The next day the woman was most apologetic when she discovered she had been shouting at Doris Archer, but really I was much too fed up to care. However, I would have been even more fed up, if I knew just how disastrous would be the after-effects of that accident.

I did not, in fact, find out until nearly two years after my fall, although during most of that time I suffered more than my fair share of aches and pains. The moment of revelation came in South Africa of all places, and again there was an element of humour in the incident.

Having caught Tony Shryane in a particularly good mood—just after he had received an MBE for services to radio—and persuaded him to let me have an extra-long break from recording so that I could have a holiday in South Africa, I visited some relatives and, as a special treat, they took me on a trip to a game reserve. We were in a group being shown round by a warden when we spotted a huge rhinoceros. We were told that we could go quite close up because rhinos had very bad eyesight and it would probably not see us. All was well until one of the group—an American lady—started talking quite loudly and startled the beast. Of course it charged straight for us and the warden, unnecessarily I thought afterwards, yelled at us to run for our lives. As I turned to follow instructions, I felt a tremendous pain in my ankle, my legs gave way and I collapsed in an ungainly heap. Luckily, this particular rhino had very bad sight and he lumbered straight ahead without noticing me on the ground.

When I was helped to my feet, my ankle still hurt but I thought it was just a sprain from the way I had twisted round. But my relatives took me to see a doctor, who insisted on an X-ray. It was that X-ray which showed up my problem— I had arthritis.

By the time I got back to England, the pain was pretty bad. It was rheumatoid arthritis and it felt as if there were broken glass cutting into my knee. I could not walk. At the same time, I discovered that it was a psoriatic condition, which meant I also had unsightly skin complications, with break-outs all over the place, including in my scalp.

It was terrible and I became frightened that I was going to be the next to disappear from The Archers. I did not want that to happen so I decided that, whatever the consequences, I would carry on as long as possible. I dragged myself to the studio in Birmingham and as I was being helped up the two flights of stairs, I suddenly thought: 'My God! This is just what it was like with Harry Oakes.' I nearly gave up then because I remembered what had happened to him through carrying on despite illness.

I still do not know why I did not give up. I said in a magazine later that I was determined 'to carry on being Doris Archer because I knew she was the kind of character who would have carried on regardless and I didn't want to let down our millions of listeners'. But I suspect such altruism. At this distance, I think it was more likely the fear of losing my status—I did not want to return to obscurity—that drove me on.

The consequence was that, just like Harry Oakes, I collapsed and had to go into hospital. I had to stay there for five weeks and that could well have been the end of my career, if it had not been for Tony Shryane and the BBC. On previous occasions, when both Harry and I had been ill, recordings had been made at our homes. This time, Tony went one further—he brought some of the cast and all the necessary gear to the hospital. No one could have asked for better therapy. It was wonderful and I have no doubt that Tony Shryane's kindness and encouragement at that time helped me to face all the pain and disability. It made me realize how lucky I was to have such an interesting job and such caring people around me. I always used to wonder what it would have been like, as is sadly the case for all too many arthritis sufferers, to be at home on one's own all day with little hope of any relief from either the pain or the monotony of loneliness. It was a time for counting blessings and when I assessed my position, it was clear that—despite everything—I still had a healthy credit balance.

After what seemed like two lifetimes, I was eventually allowed to leave the hospital and go back home. If, at the back of my mind, I thought getting away from the crisp uniforms and the smell of ether meant the end of my troubles, I was mistaken. Arthritis is not one of the illnesses one can leave behind: my worries were only just beginning.

For those lucky enough not to know too much about it, rheumatoid arthritis is a chronic and generally progressive disease that can affect any of the body's joints. Although it has been around for a long time—there was evidence of it in the skeleton of a Neanderthal man dating from forty thousand years BC—not a great deal is known about its causes and no treatment has yet been found effectively to control it. But I can tell you that what happens when you have it is that the disease causes inflammation, which in turn causes thin sheets of tissue to grow over the surface of the cartilage. Depending on the severity of the disease, that tissue and the fluid it creates can erode the cartilage and so diminish its cushioning effect between the bone-ends. That is where most of the pain comes.

At first, I could hardly move at all, and when I did it was agony. Slowly I was able to stumble around with the aid of a very clumsy walking frame. I found it all very frustrating but at least it was an awful lot better than being confined to bed or wheelchair. When I was not crying, I was giving thanks for the wonderful things I still had. And, of course, the most wonderful thing of all was The Archers. It was only in relationship to my illness that I could really see how important the programme had become to me. In my troubled time, everyone had gathered around me just like a real family. No one worried about blurring lines between fact and fantasy. When I needed love, each and every one of them gave me that. When I needed sympathy, it was there at once. And when I got really grumpy and miserable, there was always somebody able to shake me out of my pathetic self-pity.

I cannot begin to thank them enough for all they did for me. Perhaps the one way I can adequately express my gratitude is to follow their example and to hold out a hand to other arthritis victims and offer them hope.

I know that when you first feel the terrible, constant pain of arthritis, you think you will not be able to bear it. You possibly do not want to bear it, you might prefer to die. I nearly did when, at one stage, I was given the wrong treatment for the psoriasis. Somehow I survived and I can tell you now that I am glad to be alive whatever happens. Although I have often been depressed, I have still been glad to be alive to feel the pain. You do learn to live with it. I did.

While I had been somewhat wallowing in self-pity, the programme received a blow every bit as shattering as the death of Harry Oakes, although it did not hit me in quite the same way. Geoffrey Webb, one of the scriptwriters, was killed in a terrible road accident. Geoff, who had helped to create The Archers with Ted Mason and Godfrey Baseley, had been ill for some time but had almost fully recovered when the accident happened, and in fact he was on his way back from posting his latest batch of scripts when his new car was in head-on collision with a big van. He was just forty-two.

I never knew Geoff very well because, although he was often around the studio when we were recording, he was quite a shy man who seemed to keep to himself most of the time. On the few occasions we had talked, I got the feeling that he was not too comfortable with actors. He had been a journalist and I think we may have been too airy-fairy for him.

But if I did not know him all that well, he must have known me inside out, and of course he certainly knew Doris Archer even better than

I did. With Ted Mason, he had taken the embryo characters created by Godfrey Baseley and had developed them into such positive personalities that when we added our performances they became as real to millions of listeners. And, as I mentioned before, he had used quite a few of my Gwen Berryman traits in putting life into Doris Archer, so his direct influence in allowing me to perform easier, and therefore better, could not be underestimated. I am sad to say that I, like most of us in the cast I suspect, had rather taken his efforts on our behalf too much for granted, up until then.

One of the side-effects of Geoff's death was to put my health problems in perspective, and as soon as I was mobile, I went back to work and tried to carry on as near normally as possible.

I took on my fair share of the personal appearances that were still very much expected of The Archers characters. One of these was a particularly exhausting, day-long visit to the Royal Show at Stoneleigh in Warwickshire and I think it was probably one of the toughest tests I could have faced.

The Royal is an enormous show—one of the most important on the agricultural calendar—and attracts thousands of visitors. It had been decided that we would combine programme recordings with our promotional activities. So, with me in my Sunday-best, we bowled up to the showground with all the recording equipment and microphones. I was staggered when I saw the size of the place and the crowds. I had been thinking of the average kind of agricultural show and the scale of the Royal took my breath away. I think if I had really been Doris Archer from the little village of Ambridge, I would have been even more surprised: the rows of exhibits of every kind of farm machinery and equipment seemed to go on forever and there were whole herds of animals.

The organizers of the show were very efficient and when they saw me looking worried about getting mud on my shoes they immediately provided me with polythene bags, which, if they were not exactly glamorous, were effective. They were not so helpful when it came to the animals. I have already admitted to being frightened of cows, but on this occasion I had to pose with a huge bull and I was terrified: they all thought it was very funny. Luckily Bill Payne (who played Ned Larkin) was with us and, as an ex-ploughboy, he was quite at home with the beast and managed to allay my worst fears.

It was a long, tiring day, but me and my creaky joints came through with flying colours. Sadly I cannot say the same of another 'royal' occasion a few months later—and that was my first meeting with Royalty.

I was invited to a reception, at the Royal Commonwealth Society headquarters in London, which was to raise money and publicize the national Freedom-from-Hunger campaign in aid of the developing countries. I had arranged a collection among the cast and I had a cheque for about thirty pounds to present to the Queen Mother. There was quite a large group of famous women also there to make their contributions—Lady Douglas-Home, Mrs Reginald Maudling, Mrs 'Rab' Butler, Millicent Martin, Mrs Harry Secombe, Jessie Matthews and Lady Attlee, among many others.

I was awaiting my turn when Jessie Matthews went forward with her cheque, and I could not help having a quiet chuckle to myself when the Queen Mother's aide introduced her as Lady Attlee. Jessie was, of course, Mrs Dale, in that other radio soap opera and I cattily thought the mix-up was an indication of its popularity compared to The Archers! But always the professional, Jessie ignored the mistake and made a beautiful curtsey.

When it was my turn to meet the Queen Mother—who, I remember, was wearing a beautiful, peacock-blue velvet coat and a gorgeous feathered hat—I smiled, handed over the cheque and dipped into what started as a graceful curtsey. But it stopped half-way, and then my wretched arthritic joints locked in place and I could not get back up again. Agonizing as the pain was, it felt slight alongside my anguish at the embarrassment of my predicament. All sorts of terrible thoughts flashed through my mind—that this was the end, my career was over, I would never take another bow. I felt everyone must be staring at me, pitying me, and what would Mrs Dale be thinking?

The reality was that no one had time to notice anything, thanks to the Queen Mother. With her most radiant smile, she leaned forward and grasped my hand as if in normal greeting, but then she applied a little extra pressure and sort of tugged upwards. The stubbornly-locked joints melted under the regal charm and suddenly I was upright again, with not a word said about my problem. Instead, she chatted about The Archers and how much pleasure the programme gave to so many listeners. She made it quite clear that she was a fairly regular listener and asked me to pass on her good wishes to all the other members of the cast. If I had not already been an ardent admirer of all the Royal Family, I would happily have sworn an oath of allegiance on the spot!

I was reminded of that occasion the following year when I met Jessie Matthews during a party for the casts of *Mrs Dale's Diary* and The Archers, but I am ashamed to say I did not have the courage to admit my feelings when she had been wrongly introduced. It was probably just as well because I put my foot in it and upset her by saying I was not a fan of *Mrs Dale's Diary* after she had said she listened every week to the omnibus edition of The Archers.

The party was another piece of shrewd publicity management by the BBC and it had been arranged, ostensibly, for the cast of the London-based series to welcome us to Broadcasting House while our own studio in Birmingham was being refurbished. (This was very convenient for me because I had, a short time before, moved to London where I had bought a flat.) Needless to say, there were plenty of reporters and photographers in attendance. When one of the journalists asked me if I listened to the Dales regularly, I said honestly, but without really thinking, that I never remembered to put the programme on because when I was at home I was usually too busy doing my housework.

Jessie did not actually say anything, but then she did not need to. I knew that I had been very rude. She got her own back when it came to the photographs. We were taken out into the street and asked to walk along Portland Place with each other. She was tall and elegant, with a dancer's grace, and photographed beautifully alongside the small, plump figure leaning heavily on a walking-stick to take the strain off her arthritic knees. I looked every inch the country cousin of the almost inevitable newspaper headlines.

Although I am sure it was not meant to, that party also served as yet another reminder of our transience as popular public figures. Jessie

Matthews had not long taken over the role of Mrs Dale from Ellis Powell, who had played it for more than fourteen years. Although Ellis had been tremendously popular and there had been some public fuss when she was dropped, Jessie was already totally accepted as the new heroine.

If it hadn't been for the pain from my arthritis, I think I might have suffered a bit from knocking knees. I had no way of knowing then that I was not even half-way through my stint as Doris Archer. Insecurity still reigned over all.

CHAPTER TEN

As television became more and more popular, there was a steady drift from radio listening to television watching and in 1965, for the first time—probably because there were now so many more 'stars' to write about—we seemed to lose our position as the press's favourite show-business story. When we *were* reported, there were little knocks—all that happened in Ambridge was that I baked cakes, made tea and nagged Dan, while the others supped ale and gossiped about each other. With reluctant self-awareness, we knew that the bloom had left our cheeks and it was a time for self-examination.

Someone in the BBC hinted that the programme was beginning to sound tired and we immediately assumed that it was now only a matter of time before someone put out the light. But Godfrey Baseley and Tony Shryane did not suffer our panic. They accepted that the programme might have lost its edge and decided to do something to restore our earlier sharpness.

The first step was to tighten up the scripts, which meant I did not make so many cups of tea and the stories became more exciting. Then the screws were turned on the cast as performances were ruthlessly assessed and one or two changes made. We were given quite a lot of help, of course, and Tony Shryane managed to arrange an extra half-day's rehearsal time for us. Despite one or two groans about having to work longer hours, the actors took full advantage of this chance to polish their work.

Publicity had become an almost essential factor in nurturing The Archers and at this troubled time it was felt that some major promotional stunt was essential. The writers took the point that they had, perhaps, been getting a little too parochial and they decided to bring a breath of fresh air to Ambridge, to widen the horizons of Dan and Doris. The Archers, with their near-neighbours and friends, Fred and Betty Barratt, would go off on a holiday trip to Ireland.

Neither Monte Crick nor I took much notice

of all the plans we heard discussed, because we assumed that the holiday was another figment of the writers' imagination and that one or two Irish accents would be drafted in to bring the Emerald Isle right into the studio. I remember wondering which section of the studio floor would represent the peat bog, and whether we would have to drink real Guinness. It took Tony Shryane some time to convice us that *we* were going to Ireland—as guests of the Irish Tourist Board—and that when the listeners heard scenes set in Dublin, they really would be hearing scenes played on location there!

We were told that four of the cast would be going on the trip—Monte and me, Brenda Dunrich (Betty Barrat) and Tommy Duggan (Fred Barratt)—and we would be going three days earlier than the production team, so that we could pack in a great deal of publicity work before recording sessions for the programme.

While Tony was explaining about the publicity—there would be photographers, film cameramen and Irish television waiting for us—I was trying to work out my wardrobe and the size of the case I would need to carry all my clothes in. Before I could get round to worrying about how on earth I was going to manage to carry that with my arthritis, I suddenly realized Tony was talking about the very next Sunday, less than a week away!

I tried to control my panic, and used the train

145

journey back to London to work out the detail of my wardrobe. Normally I would have had something specially made for the occasion because being such an odd shape made it difficult to buy anything smart off the peg, but there just was not time. I decided to make do with a recently bought navy silk suit and ring the changes with different blouses and hats. Not only would I save money, but I would have a lighter load to carry across the Irish Sea.

However, having a special weakness for hats—probably thinking that, like a knickerbocker glory, the decoration on top would distract attention from what was beneath—I decided that I might be able to persuade my milliner to come up with something special. He was a young Frenchman called Claude, and he was brilliant in his use of feathers. Early next morning I rang Claude, explained about all the photographs and asked if he could create something very special. 'But of course, mademoiselle, for you I will oblige.'

A couple of days later, on the Friday morning, I was frantically packing and re-packing my suitcase when a snazzy little sports car drew up outside my flat and what looked like a huge, black hat-box with legs got out and struggled up the stairs. Inside the box, deep beneath layers of tissue paper, was a gorgeous little creation. It was a cloche covered in tiny white bobble curls made, with all Claude's skill, from goose-feathers. Each feather, he explained, had been shaped individually with curling-tongs.

I tried it on—it fitted perfectly—and I was absolutely delighted. 'Good,' said Claude, 'now I can take it away and complete my work. I will return it on Tuesday.'

Trying not to sound hysterical, I pointed out that I was leaving on Sunday and had rather wanted to take it with me. After a certain amount of Gallic histrionics and Berryman persuasion, he finally said that it might just be all right without the proper interior band. But he also gave me a dire warning: 'Please never leave it in the bathroom or the kitchen. The feathers will not much like the atmospherics.' He ignored my bewilderment and added: 'Mademoiselle should perhaps take a gold safety pin in case the catastrophe should happen and emergency repairs become necessary.'

I should have taken more notice.

On the Sunday evening, the four of us arrived in Dublin to a lovely welcome from what seemed like the whole of the Irish Tourist Board, but not too much fuss and we were allowed an early night. In my hotel room, I was pleased to see that both my silk suit and my goose-feather hat had travelled well.

Monday, according to our schedule, was to be a free day, but promptly at nine o'clock two enormous black Bentleys, hired I am sure from a local undertaker, arrived—as did our hosts from the Tourist Board—at the front doors. The lobby was already full of photographers and reporters, but what was worrying me most was the sight of the large car; it was built so high off the ground. With me leaning heavily on Monte's arm, we crossed the hall and all I could think about was how on earth I was going to get up and into this blessed limousine without looking totally undignified. But there was nothing else for it, with flash bulbs popping off all around me, I clambered, like an overgrown baby, over the running board and into the back, trying to look as graceful as possible.

As I subsided into the vast expanse of the leather seat—feeling cross at what the pictures might look like in the evening papers—I then realized, to my horror, that it was going to be even more tricky getting out. I cursed my arthritis. At our next stop all I could do was to half-slide from the seat to the floor of the car, and from there ease myself out on to the pavement. It was not exactly a stately procession, and without my beautiful hat to deflect attention upwards I am sure I would have left my confidence with my dignity—on the floor of the car.

As we walked through the city, I was amazed how well known we were. We had been used to getting fan mail from Ireland since the programme had started (they are able to pick up the BBC very clearly from across the Irish Sea, from the transmitters in the north, without having to have a licence of course), but we attracted really big crowds who wanted to talk to us and to have our autographs. I was really overwhelmed at how friendly and warm they all were.

The photographers wanted to take shots of us walking through the city and so we were asked to walk up Grafton Street, with the photographers ahead of us, walking backwards. Not content with our using the pavement like ordinary mortals, we were hustled into the middle of the roadway—one of Dublin's main thoroughfares and part of a one-way traffic system. No one had thought to close the street for a few moments or even to wave down the oncoming traffic, and impatient Dublin motorists were suddenly confronted by the rear view of four strange people strolling sedately down the middle of their street. The next thing I knew was that I was sitting firmly on the bonnet of a carpet van, being hooted and sworn at. I am sure it made good pictures, but it all did little to calm my nerves. (And to cap it all, there was a newspaper strike the next day so none of the pictures was ever used. Maybe it was just as well!)

No visit to the Emerald Isle, we were assured, could really begin until we had visited what our guide assured us, in a broad Dublin brogue, was

'The fount of that for which Ireland is justly famous'. So, having manoeuvred myself off the bonnet of the van and back into our limousine, we were driven off through the waving crowds to the Guinness factory. The company chairman himself, Viscount Elmdon, was waiting to greet us.

He must have been amazed and a little shocked to see me edging myself towards him on my bottom across the floor of our limousine and over the sill until I was sitting on the running board from which he was kind enough to help me to my feet. Politely making no reference to the odd manner of my arrival, he escorted us into the factory, where we were all invited to draw a glass for ourselves, from the barrel. It was my first-ever experience of the Irish national brew and I thought it was cool and delicious. Brenda Dunrich, who was Australian, regarded us all with a measure of distaste. As a teetotaller she had declined even a sip, and although I made it obvious that I thought she was missing out on a pleasurable experience, she would not be persuaded.

Before lunch, we were taken on a tour of the factory—through the great vat-houses, malting rooms, the steaming fermentation chambers and all the other stages of brewing. It was tiring but fascinating and I was thoroughly enjoying myself, until I felt my hat slipping down over one ear. My hat! I remembered Claude's warning: 'Please never leave it in the bathroom . . . it will not like the atmospherics.' I hurriedly excused myself and rushed into the ladies' loo, where one look in the mirror told me the worst while the goose-feathers had weathered the steaming factory, the cloche base had gone all peculiar and the hat had stretched.

Nor did I have the gold pin that Claude had suggested. There was only one thing for it—loo paper. I rolled sheets of the stuff into little balls and stuffed them into my hat and then perched it back on my head. It looked fine in the mirror and I returned to the rest of the party feeling smug about my ingenuity.

At lunch I was in the place of honour by Lord Elmdon when I became aware of a rustling noise coming from my hat and realized that the loo paper—not exactly the soft tissue kind—was unrolling, which, from where I sat, sounded almost like gunfire. If his lordship heard he was far too polite to comment. All through the soup and the fish course I hardly dared move my head for fear of unsettling the whole edifice. Unhelpfully, Monte Crick asked if I had a stiff neck and was treated to one of my most withering looks. It shut him up, for five minutes. Then, in an astonished voice, he said: 'You've got loo paper down the side of your face!'

There was nothing I could do, the ground just would not open up and swallow me. I suffered.

Even today, the Guinness advertisements can make me blush!

From the Guinness factory we went—I slunk off—to the Irish television studios where Monte and I were to be interviewed for the evening magazine programme. I had hardly been there for two minutes when the director suggested I take off my hat. I thought he had heard about my loo paper and made it clear I was not amused. But he persisted and the suggestion became a request, with the explanation that white surfaces can cause a 'flare-up' on the electronic camera. I am afraid my pride overcame professionalism and I persisted in my refusal to take off my hat. He, poor man, must have thought I was just another awkward, temperamental actress with an inflated sense of my own importance. I just did not want to spill toilet paper all over his studio floor.

All my days in Ireland were not as bad as that. We had a lovely time at Killarney, where someone introduced me to Gaelic coffee but let me think it was non-alcoholic so that I got rather fond of it. We drove north through the beautiful Irish countryside, across the border into Ulster and on to Belfast, where we paid a well-publicized visit to a folk museum, and then along the Antrim coast to Portaferry, a lovely little fishing village, where we recorded scenes for the programme in the local bar.

Everywhere the hospitality was generous and

the entertainment delightful: in the Portaferry bar, an old man with a wooden leg sang 'The Mountains of Mourne' so soulfully that John Keir Cross, one of our scriptwriters, was reduced to tears! That was Ireland.

We loved every minute of the trip—even those embarrassing moments were alleviated by the charm of our hosts—and, so it seemed, the listeners back home enjoyed the recordings we made, enough to want to follow in our footsteps. The Irish Tourist Board reported that, as a result of our visit and all the associated publicity, it had received nearly twenty thousand extra inquiries about holidays in Ireland.

For Tony Shryane and Godfrey Baseley, all this was evidence that, despite the growing menace of television, we still had plenty of pulling power; and those who had worried about the light being put out were delighted to have been proved wrong.

Almost as we set foot back in England, a row blew up among the politicians, which, I think, was further indication of the programme's continuing popularity. The trouble started with one of our 'topical inserts'. These were Godfrey Baseley's devices for keeping the programme up to date and had been introduced when the recordings were moved back six or seven weeks from the actual broadcast to accommodate overseas listeners. How they worked was that if

153

anything important or interesting happened after we had made a recording, Godfrey would get the writers to produce a new scene incorporating the up-to-date information, some of us would be rushed into the studio and the new dialogue would then be substituted for the old.

It usually worked very well and obviously helped perpetuate the realism that was so important to The Archers. For example, it gave us a better-than-normal chance of coping with the vagaries of the British weather. Nobody could foresee droughts or rainstorms and yet both are very important in agriculture and essential talking-points in any rural community. With our topical inserts, we could be having realistic conversations at almost the same time as farmers up and down the country were bemoaning their luck.

The insert that caused all the bother was not, however, about the weather, but probably the next most constant moan: the cost of beer and cigarettes. Godfrey decided that it would be very effective if he had Dan Archer and one or two of the other Ambridge locals talking about the budget on the same day as its details were announced in the House of Commons. So he got Monte Crick, Denis Folwell (who played Jack) and Bill Payne (Ned Larkin) into the studio on the Tuesday afternoon, while he and Ted Mason listened to the Chancellor's speech live on the radio. Then they hurriedly put together a script in which the locals reacted to the proposals. Within an hour or so of the Chancellor sitting down, and before many of them had heard the details, listeners to The Archers found Dan complaining about an extra penny on a pint of beer and an increase in tobacco tax.

It was probably how the majority of the country would have felt, but it outraged a Labour MP who complained that we were blatantly biased against the Government. He told the press that the BBC was 'in serious breach of its duty to deal impartially with controversial issues' and he asked the Postmaster-General (Anthony Wedgwood Benn) to direct the BBC 'under section 14 (4) of its Licence and Agreement, to drop views on public policy which have no foundation in fact' from programmes like The Archers.

Other than repeating that the BBC had a duty to treat controversial subjects with due impartiality, Mr Wedgwood Benn took no further action. But the press, reminding us of the influence of The Archers, went on worrying at our heels for several days and one of the Sunday heavyweights went as far as investigating the politics of Ambridge—and I discovered for the first time, rather late in the day you might think, that Doris Archer was a right-wing Tory.

I do not know whether or not the listeners

knew about Doris's strong views, but the scriptwriters never let me into the secret. In the fourteen years that the programme had been running, I could not recall a single conversation that would give any indication as to what Doris thought about politics, unless, of course, nagging is the preserve of the right! But according to the newspaper, 'Dan Archer is a right-wing Tory, because his father was—and Doris goes along with him.' Male-chauvinism might not have been invented then, but it was certainly alive and well.

Godfrey Baseley was quoted as agreeing that the characters held political views and said that this was essential if they were to be more than cardboard cut-outs. He then stressed that balance was maintained by Philip Archer being 'a semi-intellectual socialist'; Jack was a floating voter; Ned Larkin was left-wing; and Walter Gabriel was a Liberal.

This, of course, was not the first—or last—complaint against alleged bias in The Archers, but to me it served to show that we were still a very important element of British broadcasting. If we had not been very popular—and therefore possibly influential—the politicians would not have taken us seriously enough to care what we were saying in the Bull in Ambridge.

CHAPTER ELEVEN

As we passed the fifteenth anniversary of the programme—on 1 January, 1966—my health and temper took another turn for the worse. The arthritis was by now in both legs and both hands and I found it very difficult to get to and from the studio. Even when I was there I could not move about very much and I know I must have been a blessed nuisance to everybody. But none of them showed it. In fact, I just became more and more aware of a lovely, comforting, family feeling. When I was uncomfortable standing up—as was normal to do my recording—Tony Shryane rushed in with a chair for me to sit on and had a microphone adjusted to the new height. The dialogue in the scripts was altered so that I did not have to move around so much: Doris spent even more time in the kitchen and never ever went straight from there out to the farmyard. Whenever it was essential for Doris to be heard walking from one place to another someone else would do my footsteps and then the recording would be stopped while I shuffled into the right position and off we would go again.

I never once saw any of the cast or the production staff get irritated by the extra demands I was making on them and that stopped me from letting my own anger and frustration get completely on top of me. I was in constant pain and sometimes in absolute agony and my mood swung between self-pity and anger. I used to worry that it would show in Doris's voice when I was recording, but Tony Shryane, who was a perfectionist when it came to getting the programme right, always assured me that my voice sounded fine. And it is true that few people outside knew anything about my problems.

Things were, however, wearing me down and I was deteriorating so badly that my doctor said that if I did not stop working soon, I would be permanently crippled within three months. It was a very sobering moment and I have to confess that I did not need any second thoughts about what to do. My professional instinct to soldier on—in the-show-must-go-on tradition—must have been stifled even before it reached my conscious mind. I do not think I gave too much thought to the listeners, who were so loyal that they complained very strongly when I was not in one of the special anniversary episodes. I just took my doctor's advice. I stopped working for three months and had special treatment and drugs.

Being away from work for such a long time created two main problems for me: it cut me off from most of my friends and colleagues, and it caused me to put on weight! My greatest pleasure in life was to go out to dinner in good company. I was not much bothered about drinking—the odd glass or two of sherry was usually enough for me—but I did enjoy my food, and even more, I loved talking. The arthritis robbed me of both for a while and so I sat around doing little but stuff myself with chocolate, one of my weaknesses. I got frustrated and fat.

When I eventually got back to the studio I'm sure I must have tried everybody's patience: I chattered away almost non-stop. I always was a chatterbox but even the patient Tony Shryane admits he had a struggle to cope with me at this period. I did not realize it, but having been starved of conversation for a while, I was trying to catch up on all the gossip and went rattling on so much that I held up the recording on more than one occasion. It was all very unprofessional, I knew, but it did not seem that way at the time. I felt that I was coming back into the bosom of the family and I suppose I was going through one of those confusing periods when Gwen and Doris merged. I certainly had a good excuse for wanting to submerge my own self in the fiction of Ambridge. Doris Archer was in good health and was not afflicted by the pain and discomfort of arthritis. In fact she was described as being 'tough as old oak' and had not been known to be confined to bed with a day's serious illness in her life (not until I came along, that is, and then the poor soul had to go sick every now and then to cover my absence from the programme).

It was Doris Archer, I suspect, who helped me through the worst of my ill-health. I could escape into her quite regularly and, at least for a short period, I could leave all the agony behind. And through her, I had access to a lovely big family—husband, children, grandchildren and the prospect of great-grandchildren in the not too distant future, who all treated me as someone special. Surrogate mothers were part of the agricultural scene for orphaned animals, so what was wrong with a surrogate family?

The family atmosphere was enhanced even more when Tony Shryane announced that he was going to marry Valerie Hodgetts, who had also been with The Archers since the beginning. We were all thrilled and delighted with the news because they were so well matched. Both were lovely young people. Tony, as I have already made clear, was always very kind and gentle and I never once saw him lose his temper in even the most trying circumstances. When the programme began, Valerie was the secretary and a quiet, shy girl. But over the years, as her confidence developed, she became one of the cornerstones of The Archers. She had an amazing organizational ability and her incredible memory for detail saved all of us on many occasions. Among her many other duties—to us it seemed as if she ran the whole BBC—Valerie was responsible for the continuity of the programme. That meant she had to ensure that nothing was allowed to happen that was inconsistent with previous events: Doris Archer should not switch from being a good cook to being indifferent about food; Dan should not become a cigarette smoker after years on a pipe, and so on. She was also the repository of information about every Archer birthday and anniversary, every Archer relative, friend and neighbour, and she kept them all in their rightful places within Ambridge. Although she obviously had files and books to help, Valerie had an astonishing memory and could answer most queries off the top of her head. (She has been a great help in writing this book, with her readiness to check dates and remind me of anecdotes.)

The wedding was further evidence of how much a family affair the programme had become—a much wider family than that which the writers had influence over. There, as Tony Shryane (producer) married Valerie Hodgetts (programme assistant), the best man was Edward J. Mason (scriptwriter) and one of the other speakers was Norman Painting (actor), who also presented Tony and Valerie with a silver salver engraved with all our autographs. And among the guests you could see the widening of the family circle as one took in the husbands and wives of those directly involved with the programme. (Today that circle is even wider and, for example includes the Shryanes' three lovely children, Elizabeth, Michael and Dominic, even though, like me, Tony is now retired from The Archers.)

Family occasions are often appropriate moments for standing back and taking stock and there were two anniversaries in 1966 that afforded me opportunities to assess both my career and my life. The first was the programme's four-thousandth episode, the second was my sixtieth birthday.

By marking both the date anniversaries (every 1 January) and all the round-figure episodes (100, 500, 1,000 and so on) the programme had had nearly as many birthdays as me and by the time we got to the four-thousandth episode in May, 1966, some sections of the press were beginning to think of The Archers as being quite old and the minor criticisms of the previous year grew into a full-blooded analysis of our prospects. For folk more used to adulation, it was all very uncomfortable.

One journalist suggested that the programme was 'winding itself up for the final curtain' and others pointed out that television was continuing to make inroads into our audience. There was, sadly, plenty of evidence for the second comment: the listening figures did show a slow, steady decline and the number of invitations for personal appearances—in the past always seen as something of a barometer of our success—was lower than before.

As insecure artistes, sometimes bordering on the paranoid, we did not really need any more evidence than that to support the first suggestion. We all knew it was only a matter of time before the gravy train ground to a halt. Even a BBC denial that any consideration had been given to taking The Archers off the air, did not much help our nervousness. We simply would not have been expected to be told much in advance if they had been toying with the idea. We had learned over the years that, important as we might have been, we could never really be taken into consideration when all the higher management decisions were being made. Nor did we suffer any undue bitterness about such a situation. We knew our place and considered ourselves very lucky to have been part of such a successful venture.

All this I can see now on standing back from the day-to-day events. Close up it was much more confusing and traumatic.

Because of my physical condition I had been very pleased not to be on television, as had once been suggested, because I knew that I would not have been able to carry on as Doris Archer. Not wanting to be part of television, I therefore did not take very much notice of it and could not quite see what all the fuss was about. I was also still making quite a few personal appearances—if they were less often than before, it was because of my arthritis—and wherever I went I was still treated like royalty. There was still a lot of fuss about me!

If that was the case, I thought, I was very important to the continuing success of The Archers, and to hear that the programme might be ending just did not make any kind of sense. It was then that the trauma began, because I suddenly realized that my sixtieth birthday was looming ahead and, without my work, I could see a sad and lonely old-age pensioner knitting her life away between bouts of pain. I had no illusions about finding other work—where would I find a producer as thoughtful and kind as Tony Shryane?—and I could not even envisage going back into business again because I could not hope to survive being on my feet around a shop most of the day. If, as earlier suggested, the light might be going out of The Archers, I had little doubt that it would be going out for Gwen Berryman too.

But, before I was consumed by such maudlin thoughts, someone put a shilling in the meter. Just as quickly as the fears decended, they disappeared. When the axe did not fall at the expected moment, we could not go on agonizing, so we simply rationalized the worries out of existence. And, imaginary as the dangers might have been, survival came as a victory.

One of the things that helped The Archers maintain its essential freshness was, I believe, the regular injection of energy and enthusiasm we received from the arrival of new actors and actresses. Even though the regular cast was now between twenty-five and thirty, one new face could make a difference.

At a very good psychological moment (whether or not that was planned, I don't know), Tony Shryane introduced us to a young Scots actress called Julia Mark, who was to play the new barmaid at the Bull, Nora McAuley. Despite Julia's own accent, Nora was to be Irish—no doubt as a result of our visit to the Emerald Isle—and there was another confusing dimension in that Julia was only the stage name of Margaret Rees.

The fact that Julia (or Margaret) was the wife of one of the new BBC bosses in Birmingham was a very good sign and we took it as an indicator that there must be some future for the programme. We reckoned Mr Rees would hardly have let his wife knowingly join a sinking ship.

Although we were right about the future, we were wrong about Alan Rees and what he would or would not tell Julia about his plans for The Archers. If we thought she was going to be some kind of mole who would give us access to the thinking of higher management, we were wrong. We soon learned that she was in the same boat as the rest of us and had to endure our neuroses and apprehensions. Every now and again she would get completely exasperated by her failure to pry any information from Alan, and she would swear that he did not have a single thought in his head.

Somebody in management was, however, having hard thoughts about the programme and was planning yet another controversy that would catapult us back into the headlines. An illegitimate baby was being planned!

I am sure today such an incident would hardly raise any comment, but at the time it was still something of a scandal for an unmarried girl to have a baby. I was quite shocked myself when I first heard about the storyline in which Doris's granddaughter, Jennifer, would become pregnant, refuse to name the father but insist on having the child and bringing it up herself. I think this was one of the occasions when I identified very closely with Doris Archer. I forgot for a while that the whole thing was a fiction and when I saw (later) what Doris was writing in her 'diary', published by the BBC in 1972, it summed up how I might have felt if it had been real:

I just couldn't believe it when young Jennifer told me she was going to have a baby. It just didn't seem possible. I've always thought of her as a sweet, innocent child. It's difficult to realize she's in fact twenty-one and a very mature woman now.

The lass was terribly upset, hadn't been able to tell her mum and dad, and I don't think I was a big help to her. I honestly don't remember exactly what I said. I was so shocked. I know I felt ashamed and kept saying to myself that it couldn't happen in the Archer family. In other people's families yes, but not in ours. I hope I didn't say that to Jennifer.

My first instinct was that she must get married right away but she said she couldn't. The father didn't love her and she didn't mean anything to him. I tried to persuade her but she wouldn't have anything to do with the idea and point-blank refused to say who the father was. I got a bit angry then because when girls take that line it's usually because they don't know exactly who is the father.

It was disgraceful of me, I know. Young Jennifer isn't a trollop and I had all but suggested it. No wonder she rushed off crying. I felt so ashamed. She had come to me for help and all I could do was feel sorry for myself and the Archer family.

I suppose it's because I don't understand the young people of today. They look as if they never wash, have long hair, wear dirty old jeans and they've absolutely no morals at all! You've only got to watch television or read the papers to see what I mean. Not that I would have included our Jennifer in that lot.

The thing that brought me to my senses about it all was our Jack's reaction. He was livid and all he could think of was turning the poor mite out into the street. He ranted and raved so much that Dan got angry and said maybe Jack would be happier if Jennifer just did away with herself and then she wouldn't be an embarrassment.

It was a horrifying moment but I'm ever so grateful to Dan. It was him who made us realize it was a human being—our own flesh and blood—we were discussing. He's a good man, Dan Archer. Now we can forget about shame and embarrassment and get on with helping the lass. She's certainly going to need it.

Being an unmarried mother is bad enough anywhere but in a small community like Ambridge it's even worse. Everyone knows each other and each other's business. If our Jennifer is prepared to face all the gossip among her own friends then she's a brave girl and deserves our support.

The reaction of the listeners was, of course, mixed. There were those who were horrified: what was Ambridge coming to with such goings on? And they complained that the subject was not suited to family audiences. There were others who saw the positive side of the story and how it brought the best out of the family. In the

House of Lords, Baroness Serota said that Doris Archer's response to a difficult situation had represented 'a sensitive and courageous' step by the BBC. Because I agreed so much with Doris's attitude, I took the Baroness's remarks as something of a personal compliment!

Whatever their views, nearly everyone was intrigued about the mystery of the father. One of the documentary producers at the BBC told me that when he went to the directors' dining-room of a big industrial organization to discuss the state of British industry, he ended up being quizzed about who was the father for nearly two hours. June Spencer (Peggy) recalled how her little girl was called away from her ballet lessons to be questioned on the subject by the proprietress of the school—Dame Marie Rambert!

By way of capitalizing on the success of that particular storyline, Tony Shryane and Godfrey Baseley launched us on another great promotional tour, this time to Scotland.

Having learned from my Irish adventures, I was determined not to take any chances in the far north and so I travelled with bags that were lighter for being without goose-feathers.

We had a wonderful time and after we made recordings in Inverness, Monte Crick was measured for a kilt and no one would tell me what a Scotsman did or did not wear underneath. We went to Loch Ness to look for the monster but only found an old man who swore he had seen it and spoke with such eloquent conviction that I believed him, for an hour or so anyway.

In Aberdeen, I had one of the most humbling moments of my life. When we arrived at the Granite City's railway station, I was approached by an old lady who told me she had been waiting for hours to meet Doris Archer so that she could say how much she enjoyed listening to her on the wireless. I was quite touched by the woman's obvious sincerity, but I was not ready for her next gesture. She explained that she was very poor and that she really only had one thing of any value. She wanted me to have it and use it in the kitchen at Brookfield. It was a simple butter dish. I cried and the tears rolled down my face as I tried to tell her how much the gift meant to me, much more than anything expensive might have done.

Also in Aberdeen I was dragged out of bed in the middle of the night—Tony Shryane said it was dawn—to visit the city's fish market. The cold and damp did nothing for my poor old bones or my creaky, arthritic joints. And the comments of the fish men did even less for my confidence in buying fish back home in Wolverhampton. They told me that there were several grades of fish and whatever was left of a catch after it had been sorted into first, second and third grades was then boxed and sent to the

English Midlands. 'You're so far from the sea there that you would never know the difference between good and poor fish,' they claimed.

From Aberdeen we went on to Braemar for the famous Highland Games. I tried to persuade Monte to wear his kilt and have a go at tossing the caber, but when he saw the great giants, swaggering around the place, he decided that discretion would be the better part of valour.

The Queen and several other members of the Royal Family were at the Games and I was so busy trying to get a better view of them that I nearly had a nasty accident. We had been recording a scene near the entrance to the arena, when Tony Shryane told me that the royal party had just gone to their seats. Being so small, I could not really see from where we were so I moved out into the pathway and was so concentrating on what the Queen was wearing that I did not realize I was slap bang in the way of an advancing pipe band. I do not think they could have seen me from under their great shaggy bearskins and, as panic and arthritis are not the best of companions, I just stood there waiting to be trampled underfoot. Luckily Tony and Monte saw my predicament and they rushed over to help me out of the way just in the nick of time.

The one sadness about that visit to Scotland was that we did not have the company of John Keir Cross. He had died earlier in the year after a long illness and we missed his presence very much. In Ireland, he had added a great deal of merriment to our travels and being a lovely, romantic character he had made me see so many things in a different light. What he would have been like showing us his native Scotland one can hardly imagine.

When he had joined The Archers after Geoffrey Webb's death, some of the cast got worried about the change in their characters—and there was a fair bit of Scottish influence in Ambridge, with Andrew Sinclair moving more into the foreground—but I warmed to him immediately. He was a well-known writer of thrillers and had been involved with radio, television and films long before he came to us and he was a tough, hard-drinking professional. He used to say with great glee that he overcame his wife's attempts to cut down on his drinking by keeping a bottle of whisky on a string in the stream at the bottom of his garden. I do not know if that was actually true, but it certainly fitted in with John's personality and I will believe it because I want to.

I suppose I was a bit like the listeners, described then by yet another journalist seeking the secret of our success:

It's no use telling the fans that The Archers aren't real. To the fans they are more than real. They are twice as vivid as life itself. They are a secret company of intimate friends.

It's a curious thing, this capturing of the imagination by a piece of unabashed fiction. Sometimes it is done by great art.

When *David Copperfield* first appeared in instalments, an American woman ran out of her house one dark night in lashing rain, with streaming eyes and her shawl pulled over her head, to tell a friend that Steerforth was dead.

Sometimes it is done by a startling degree by stuff that isn't great art and, in fact, isn't art at all.

That's The Archers for you. What is the secret of the immense success of this soap opera serial? You may say it's escapism. Of course it's escapism, but it's not the usual escape into high drama or luxurious and exciting living.

An elderly Oxford don was once asked what was his secret ambition. He said, 'To live in guilty splendour with a duchess.' That is one form of escapism, but there are no duchesses in the Archer family circle. The whole thing, most skilfully done, is as commonplace as the back pages of a country newspaper.

Perhaps that's the secret. We are more heavily industrialized than any other nation in the world and we have been industrialized for longer. But still we nurse the secret unconquerable dream of the simple and natural country life.

When you see a factory worker digging his allotment in the shadow of a slag heap, you see the representative type of our people. And you can be sure that his wife wouldn't miss The Archers for anything.

For which I, for one, was truly thankful.

CHAPTER TWELVE

When Harry Oakes died, in 1961, I was shocked, partly because it was so unexpected and partly because of the effect I thought it was going to have on me personally. In 1969, I knew Monte Crick was dying and I knew that arrangements were in hand to replace him as Dan Archer and yet his death came as the most terrible blow.

My relationship with Monte was never quite the same as with Harry. Monte was a much quieter man, almost shy, and he had been very conscious of taking Harry's place so that he was constantly diffident about his ability as an actor, and about his role within The Archers. He did not take naturally to the figure-head image and I felt that he had to act to cover his reluctance to be the leader.

But he was a wonderful actor and on the air he was every bit the Dan Archer, loved and respected by millions of radio listeners. He was the complete professional and I grew to respect him enormously. I also liked him very, very much. He was a very stylish man and we shared an interest in the good things of life.

I watched with delight as he fell madly in love with Anne Cullen, the beautiful young actress who played (and still does) Carol Tregorran. It was lovely to see them together, almost like a couple of teenagers, delighting in the discovery of new aspects of each other's personality. It was sad to see how distraught Monte was when Anne was ill and it was a relief to see how happy he became when she got better. It was sadder still to watch Anne being very brave as poor Monte became more and more seriously ill.

It had started off with nothing more than a sore throat—'a touch of laryngitis,' he told me—which did not seriously affect the recording sessions. Then it got worse and Dan Archer had to contract a sore throat to cover the change in Monte's voice. Sometimes he lost his voice altogether and could not record, but always it was shrugged off as a virulent throat infection that would soon get better.

When it did not, Anne insisted that he see a specialist, and that was when she learned how ill he was. He had cancer of the throat and only a few months at the most to live. She refused to tell Monte and determined to make his last days as happy as possible. We readily agreed to help keep the secret from him.

He was only away from the studio for a short

time and when he came back I acted as if there were nothing wrong. It was comparatively easy at first, but as it became more difficult for him—those wretched steep stairs at the Birmingham studio caused him agony—so it became more of a strain for us to feign normality. When you see someone in such obvious pain, it takes an awful lot of self-control not to sympathize and offer help. But if Anne could cope with the terrible helplessness, we could only try to support her.

When he simply could not get up the stairs, it was once again Tony Shryane who resolved the problems. He had a little sort of cubby-hole on the ground floor converted into a tiny studio and linked it to the main control-room. He said there were other reasons for doing this and, although I was not so sure, Monte believed him and happily went in there to record his scenes while the rest of us were upstairs, hearing him on the link line.

If Anne had not been around and being so brave, I do not know how I could have coped. It was terrible to see such a lovely man just fade slowly away. I shall never forget the last episode he was able to take part in. It was dreadful. I knew Monte saw The Archers as one of the best things that had happened in his life—it had given him a new career and a wonderful wife— and I knew that he did not want to stop working, but I found it very hard to see any real point in letting the poor man suffer so much. I just wanted to stop it all and send him home so that his wife could try to give him some comfort. I did not know it was his last recording, but that night I cried more than I have ever cried before.

Monte went into a nursing home where he died several weeks later with his wife, Anne, by his bedside. All of us grieved with her.

When we got over the shock of Monte's death, I was once again faced with the problem of getting to know the new Dan Archer—the third—Edgar Harrison. And just as before, I was frightened of the prospect. I knew that the Dan-Doris relationship was still very important to The Archers and if, for any reason, the new actor did not get on with me, it would be bad for the programme.

I did not know very much about Edgar. He had been brought in to understudy Monte and he played one of Dan's cowmen, I think, for a few weeks. But because of the need to keep the extent of his illness from Monte, we did not really talk of Edgar as a replacement for Dan, and as Doris did not have much to do with the cowmen, I had little chance to get to know him before he took over the part properly.

I know it seems daft for me to be frightened, after all I was the one on home ground, but I really was scared of meeting Edgar. When we were introduced, I felt all flustered and the poor man must have wondered what on earth he had

177

let himself in for when he was confronted with a far-from-friendly woman, whom he might rightly have expected to welcome him with open arms.

It was a very odd feeling for me. I do not have the experience to be certain, but I suppose it was a bit like acquiring a new husband without having any say in the matter and without any courtship. Who would have been happy in that situation? It was not something that I could talk to the man himself about, because he would have thought I was dotty to get so worked up about a simple change of casting. It happened in the theatre every day.

But just as Monte had done, so Edgar slowly settled into the role. Coming from Bristol, his natural voice was beautifully rounded with the soft west country accent, but when he was on microphone he sounded uncannily like Monte's Dan Archer. In fact, when she heard the two of them on tape, Edgar's wife said she could not tell them apart, and that was after thirty-five years of marriage!

Despite the voice, however, I could not take to Edgar at first. (I'm speaking now of him as Dan, not Edgar.) I think it had something to do with age. Maybe it was because he made me aware of my own advancing years—I was sixty-three. I had aged alongside Monte and consequently never noticed that he and I were both getting on a bit. Suddenly the new man comes along and I could see he was older than I had ever seen Monte. The fact that he was about a year or so younger than me did not count.

It was all very irrational and I soon got over it as I got to know Edgar a bit better. Like me, he had not thought about an acting career when he left school. He went into the insurance business and it was not until after many years in amateur theatricals that he decided to turn professional. I think it was when he started to tell me stories about his days in the theatre that I grew to like him. One of his tales was about a production of *The Scarlet Pimpernel* in which he played opposite Phyllis Neilson-Terry. The great lady forgot one of her lines and Edgar did a bit of ad-libbing until she got back on the rails. Afterwards, when she was thanking him for helping her out of the professional's most embarrassing predicament, she said: 'Thank heavens I wasn't playing that scene with one of those amateurs.' Edgar said he could not then admit the truth—it was only his second paid performance.

Hard on Edgar's arrival, events in the programme's storyline took a turn that also underlined age—Dan and Doris gave up Brookfield Farm to move into Glebe Cottage. It was a traumatic period for them both, Dan ending a lifetime as a farmer, giving up his land to his son, acknowledging the end of his working life; Doris leaving the only home she and Dan had known together, acknowledging that at seventy (she was older than me), she could not really cope any more with being the hard-working wife of a farmer.

I was able to identify very much with Doris as she first faced and then made the move. When my father died, he had left me his large house in Wolverhampton and I had enjoyed building up a collection of antiques there and had revelled in the freedom of the two-acre garden—growing vegetables there had been the nearest I ever got to an agricultural experience. It was a real home. But it was much too big for me and I eventually had to leave to move into a smaller place. It was a very unhappy feeling—endings always make me like that—and I suspect that is one of the reasons I have moved from house to flat and from flat to flat quite regularly ever since; a reluctance to put down roots too deeply because of the agony of pulling them up.

As if all that was not miserable enough for anyone, I contracted Bell's Palsy on top of the arthritis. I had been away for a short holiday and had come back for the celebrations to mark the programme's five-thousandth episode, when the palsy hit me and my face collapsed horribly into a terrible distortion. It felt like the last straw: I was by now using a stout walking-stick to support my arthritic knees and I was having more scalp trouble from psoriasis. My sense of humour was sorely tested and I nearly gave up so that, like Doris, I could retire to a country cottage and hide myself away from everybody.

I didn't. I bought a new evening dress, pretended that my fairy godmother had, Cinderella-like, waved a magic wand to make me beautiful and I went to the ball. The 'ball' was a lovely party, this time given by the cast and production staff, at which we were hosts to all the senior BBC people including the Director-General. What they must have thought of me, all dolled up but leaning on a heavy stick and having great difficulty in talking and even more trouble in eating, heaven only knows. I must have looked quite bizarre. Still, I was there, and for me that was the main thing. If I could not really join in with the fun, I could watch and get great pleasure from seeing everyone else enjoying themselves. I was still part of it all and my word I got a lot of fuss and attention. I was so glad I had not been silly and stayed at home.

Staying at home was not really part of my nature. I had always been gregarious, even as a child, and as soon as the palsy cleared up I went off for another holiday, this time to Italy. Probably because of my opera training and all those years of dreaming about curtain calls at La Scala, Milan, I had a special affection for the country and the wonderfully musical language. I had not learned to *speak* Italian at the Academy but I could sing lots of wonderfully romantic songs as fluently as a native. On one previous holiday, I became friendly with a young couple—they were hairdressers—and used to sing for them in their salon while I was having my hair done. At the end of the holiday, I gave them a little bunch of flowers each and, in traditional Latin-style, we cried all over each other as we said our farewells. I knew their names were Emi and Marissa, but I had not understood much else of what they had said during the whole fortnight.

I had resolved to learn Italian before I went back there again, and in fulfilment of my ambition I bought all the BBC language records and watched all the special programmes, *Si Dice Cosi*, on television on Sunday mornings. I even gave up the omnibus edition of The Archers in my pursuit of perfection. Just before this particular holiday, I was convinced that I had succeeded because I could mimic all the voices on the records with total accuracy. During the journey to a lovely little resort near Genoa, I practised endlessly and thought I was doing well from the generous smiles of airline hostesses, taxi drivers, porters and so on. In my hotel room, I decided to surprise Emi and Marissa, so I rang downstairs and in my now impeccable Italian, asked for an appointment to be made at their salon. There was a long silence at the end of my request. It was the proprietor himself. 'Scusa, signorina, please speak in your lovely

English and I understand you very well. Be cruel to my lovely Italian and I not understand what you talk about!' All those hours sweating over a hot record-player wasted.

But it did not stop me enjoying my holiday, the highlight of which was an appearance on the stage of La Scala, Milan. Alas, not—in fulfilment of my dream—during a performance, but after a spell-binding production of Mozart's *Il Ralto dal Serraglio*. There were so many curtain calls that I lost count and my poor arthritic hands ached as I tried to keep up with the ecstatic Italians. I learned later, to my horror, that the performers had a good idea of the number of curtain calls before they went on stage, because they had more or less paid for them. I had been vaguely aware of the 'claque' but did not know how it operated. Bluntly speaking, they are a group of up-market cheer leaders who, for a fee, will enthuse any audience into rapturous applause. It was carefully explained to me that, of course, they would not undertake their duties unless the company was of the highest order. 'They will not try to make a bad performance good, but they can make a great performance seem magnificent,' I was told. I wondered if anyone had been paid to clap at my first performance in Wolverhampton many moons earlier. I would not have put it past my doting parents.

It was the English singer, Elizabeth

Harwood, who invited me backstage after the performance. I knew her from having been at the Royal Academy of Music at the same time as her mother, and she introduced Michael Heltan and Elke Schary and Maestro Romano Gondolfi, and let me walk across the stage. The curtain was down and the audience had gone home but I could still hear the applause and, for just a moment or two, it was for me.

Back home in England, I trod my own set of boards and found to my joy that my own kind of applause really was still there for me. Edgar and I were invited to make a personal appearance at the harvest festival in Hanbury Parish Church (the one we used as Ambridge's own), and when we walked in with the vicar the whole congregation spontaneously got to its feet and all the necks craned as people tried to get a better view of us. It might not have matched the rapture of the audience reaction at La Scala, but I knew there was no claque in Hanbury. The warmth of their response was stimulated only by genuine affection for The Archers. It was nice to know it was still there. It felt like old times and, of course, I cried.

I smiled when I saw another kind of reaction to the programme. Going through London in a taxi one day, I saw, painted in huge scrawl across a bridge, the slogan: 'Doris Archer is a prude!' Though I had not bargained for such a splash of recognition, it did show that my performance had made somebody think.

One listener found a better way of telling me what she thought of my performance as Doris Archer. Dutifully, every month for nearly a year, she carefully wrapped a little gift and sent it to me in a buff-coloured envelope. It was a chocolate biscuit. From the scribbled notes that accompanied each biscuit, it was clear that the sender was very old and very lonely. She said she listened to us all the time and felt that the Archers were a real family, and for those few minutes she had a sense of belonging. It was a comfort to her in her loneliness. Her biscuit was worth its weight in gold to me.

These incidents were, in fact, evidence of the amazing endurance of the programme. While it was evoking affection and contempt, there must, I felt, be plenty of life left in it.

A journalist asked me at the time just why I thought we had survived when Mrs Dale and her friends had been taken off the air. I am still quite pleased with my reply: 'It's because we deal far more with ordinary life. The Dales were really for people who, at the time it went out in the afternoon, sat and listened to it as they poured tea from a silver teapot!'

In the same interview, which described me as 'buxom', I also said I would like to go on as long as people wanted me.

CHAPTER THIRTEEN

There were all sorts of changes going on at the BBC as we came up to the twentieth anniversary of the programme—on 1 January 1971—and the overall effect was to leave most of us in the cast feeling distinctly apprehensive about our future.

In the great scheme of things, it seemed that there was little part for The Archers. Management changes in Birmingham meant we had a new boss and we learned that he did not see us as an important part of his responsibilities. He was even reported to be resentful of our programme because it had knocked his boyhood hero, Dick Barton, off the air.

For all the previous years, we had been used to a special relationship with the Corporation's managers and this had given us a sense of importance. To discover that we were part of just another programme was very disconcerting. When the new man, a young Scotsman called Jock Gallagher, told us that it had been decided not to celebrate the twentieth anniversary, we assumed the worst—the programme was to be taken off. We reckoned that the BBC did not want to waste money on parties and things when they were shortly going to kill us all off. It was the only explanation we could think of for such a drastic change in an organization that had so enthusiastically marked all our previous milestones.

The self-confidence that we had previously enjoyed, because of our tremendous popularity with listeners, had already been dented by the serious illness of two very important members of the team—Denis Folwell, who played Jack Archer, and Edward J. Mason, who had written most of our scripts over the twenty years. The new reverse—that is how it looked to us—came as a real body blow and even the usually-exuberant Godfrey Baseley seemed subdued. We had worried unnecessarily about previous false alarms, but this time we could see the white of the marksman's eye as he peered down the telescopic sights at his sitting-duck target.

While we were sitting thus transfixed, both Ted Mason and Denis Folwell died and any concerns about our careers were submerged in grief. Both men had been with us since the beginning and in twenty years we had all become close friends.

Ted Mason's contribution to The Archers was all but impossible to measure. He had been called in by Godfrey Baseley to create the characters and to write the first script. It was his skill with the pen that had given the actors and actresses the words and characterizations that had allowed us to establish such a realistic picture for the listeners. He was not a

187

countryman—in fact he was born and bred in Birmingham and had worked in a city factory before becoming a full-time writer—but he had a beautifully-sensitive understanding of rural life and you could always tell when you were reading one of his scripts.

I was not aware of it at the time because Ted did not talk to us much about it, but he fought regular battles within the BBC to be allowed to keep our dialogue and storyline up to date, and it was largely through his efforts that The Archers avoided the perils of falling behind the times and fossilizing.

But, of course, his contribution is not measured only on quality but also on quantity. It is one thing to maintain standards, another to maintain them day in day out for twenty years. Someone worked out that he had written more than half of all the scripts—somewhere around 2,700—and that that had been more than six and a half million words. Having tried to put together a tiny fraction of that for this book, I can only marvel at the feat.

We still hadn't got used to the idea that Ted had gone when Denis Folwell died. In the programme, Denis played my son—although he was a couple of years older than me—and we had therefore grown very close to each other. I had seen him burn the candle at both ends for several years but had never been able to persuade him to be more sensible. He took about as much notice of me as any son would have done of his mother's fussing, but you could not help loving him. He had a really wicked sense of humour and he always covered up his pain and discomfort with a joke or two.

Denis, who came from Leciester, had been an actor for many years before he joined The Archers. Like me, he had been in the provincial repertory theatre but had also worked in the West End and had been a producer at one point. He started broadcasting in 1934 and for a couple of years he was Larry the Lamb in the famous Children's Hour series of *Toytown*. One of his other claims to fame was that he was the original Worzel Gummidge, the crazy scarecrow character recently revived on television by Jon Pertwee.

The writers did not help us get over Denis's death: they kept Jack alive in the programme for nearly another year. It was evidently felt that it was not a good moment to kill off the character and we therefore had the painful experience of continuing to talk about Jack for an awful long time. It was particularly difficult because they had given him much the same illness as Denis—initially to explain the change in his voice—and we had to go through a fictional deterioration after having suffered the trauma of a real one. When Jack was finally allowed to die, it felt as if we were going through Denis's death all over again. It was not a good experience.

Although in different ways, both Ted and Denis had made enormous contributions to the success of The Archers and without them we worried that the programme might have lost its soul. It must have been the lowest moment since it all began in 1951.

I must have added to the gloom because my own health took a turn for the worse and my doctor issued another of his dire warnings: if I went on working—especially climbing those awful stairs at the Birmingham studio—I would spend the rest of my life in a wheelchair.

I did not want to retire, partly because I did not like the idea of not having any work to do, but also because I desperately did not want anyone else to step into my shoes and play Doris Archer. I know it was all very irrational but that is just how I felt. In retrospect, I think I can now understand what was going on inside me at that time. No one knew better than me that Doris Archer was too important—for all sorts of reasons—to be killed off just then. It would have upset the listeners dreadfully and it would have caused an even further lowering of morale amongst the cast. Nor did anyone know better than me that re-casting was possible, because I had worked with three different Dans. But at the same time, somewhere in the very depths of my subconscious, I associated re-casting with death. If Doris Archer were replaced it would have something to do with the death of Gwen

Berryman. A wheelchair must have seemed preferable and I ignored my doctor's advice.

Luckily, the clouds started rolling back before his grim prediction became a reality. The first glimmer of hope for me came when, in 1971, we moved from the old studio in Birmingham to the BBC's new multi-million-pound centre at Pebble Mill, where our studio was on the ground floor. There were no killer stairs. Even though the canteen was on the seventh floor, there was a lift to make life easy. There were other advantages. The new building accommodated all the Birmingham staff who had previously been in offices all over the city, and once everybody was under the same roof, the general facilities improved. For example, there was a fully-equipped surgery and a full-time nursing sister. It was the nurse who made the biggest difference to me. Tony Shryane talked to her and I suddenly found that there was a wheelchair always available to get me from my car to the studio and from there to the canteen and anywhere else I wanted to go.

In the canteen, which was much bigger and brighter than the old one, we re-established our 'family circle' and the catering staff responded to my wheelchair by waiting on me hand and foot. It was lovely. I felt like a queen bee as they fussed around me, bringing my food and things while everyone else had to queue and help themselves.

That is one of the nicer things I have learned from having arthritis: people are so kind and helpful if you give them half a chance. It is important, however, to stay reasonably cheerful. People are bound to be more reluctant to do things for you if you are miserable and moaning all the time. You cannot just sink back and feel sorry for yourself. You have got to count your blessings and be grateful for things that you still can do. That is not easy for me nowadays with all my other problems on top of the arthritis, but in the early seventies I really felt that I could show an example to fellow-sufferers and I talked to various groups about how I managed. I used always to tell them that whenever I was in danger of getting really depressed, I thought back to one day in London when I got out of my car and was suddenly seized with pain. I literally could not move and I had to hang on to some railings to keep myself upright. That was very early on and I was convinced: this was the end of everything. It was not, of course, and I slowly learned that it was better just to take one day at a time. In those days I really did have hope—that the researchers would find a cure—and I wanted to share it with everyone. When I felt so much better after our move to Pebble Mill, I was glad that I had done as I preached and taken one day at a time. If I had listened to the doctor and thought about the future, I would have missed many of the excitements and joys that were then still in front of me.

And if the clouds started lifting for me personally, the same was happening with The Archers. Jock Gallagher had heard of the panic about the lack of celebrations for the twentieth birthday and he came into the studio to explain: the twentieth had only been played down because there were very special plans for the twenty-first, a coming-of-age that none of us had thought about.

Although he did not disclose any of the plans, he must have been very reassuring, for I felt confident enough to confess my own anxieties over how long I could carry on and my feeling of dread about someone else taking over the part of Doris. I knew it was a silly feeling but he seemed to understand and he made me a promise: if I carried on for as long as I could—or wanted—he would guarantee that my part would *not* be re-cast. Suddenly I saw my problems in a much better context: that I *could* turn over the pages of the script became more important than how difficult it was; and instead of worrying about being old and grey, I could look forward to being a nice, white-haired, grandmother figure. That is what confidence does for you!

The programme itself started to find its old style with a series of happenings clearly aimed at getting us back in the headlines in time for the twenty-first birthday celebrations. For example, we had the 'wedding of the year'—as the *Radio Times* labelled it—when Doris's granddaughter, Lilian, married the Squire of Ambridge, Ralph Bellamy. The 'ceremony' was recorded at Hanbury Church and we all dressed up for the occasion, the menfolk in morning suits and the women in all their finery. Outside the church afterwards, it was just like a real wedding with dozens of photographers making us all pose as their shutters clicked away noisily. The pictures appeared in most of the national papers and the *Radio Times*—always very helpful to The Archers—published a special four-page feature, including a large colour photo that reminds me that I wore a fairly strident purple outfit, suggesting my confidence was high at the time. In an article, the magazine had another shot at defining the reason for our success: 'It is the complex interaction of reality and fantasy, hard fact and wishful thinking which has made "The Archers" the most fascinating as well as the most successful radio soap opera ever.'

It went on to say how deeply involved everyone was in the programme and quotes Jock Gallagher: 'Everyone concerned is one hundred per cent committed. At first people find this a bit strange. I know I did. But when you get involved, you know you're doing something very important. In a strange, psychological way it's not fiction; it's a piece of fiction that evokes reality. It really is a mirror and we're all looking into it.'

Around that time, there were so many bridges between imagination and reality that it became bewildering. The fictional wedding recorded in a real church was followed by Dan and Doris's golden wedding in the story being commemorated outside the programme by the striking of a medallion to sell to listeners. That medallion sums up the confusion: on one side there are the heads of Dan and Doris (for which Edgar Harrison and I were the models) perpetuating the myth of a happily-married couple; on the other, there is the legend—BBC Radio Four—and that establishes the reality.

Then there was the publication of a book which was supposed to be Doris Archer's diary for the preceding twenty-one years and which was sold across the counter of all the bookshops. When one journalist found out I had not actually written a word of it, she wanted to know if I was being paid for the use of my name. I found it too awkward to point out that no one *was* using my name. At the same time, I got a bit cross when a confectionery manufacturer produced 'Doris Archer's Country Fudge' and I was asked to let them use my writing of Doris's signature without any payment being offered. When I protested, Jock Gallagher pointed out that as there was not really a Doris Archer, it did not matter much whose handwriting the signature was in. They had only asked me for the sake of consistency and out of courtesy. I signed sheepishly, having fallen into the same trap as the journalist.

I am not sure how successfully the fudge went, but the 'diary' sold something like ninety thousand copies and the medallion several thousand. What a pity there was no Doris to benefit from the royalties!

By far the most memorable of the events leading up to the twenty-first birthday was the visit we received from Princess Anne, the first royal to see a recording of the programme. The Princess visited Birmingham to open the new Pebble Mill centre officially and we were among those chosen to meet her. Thoughtful as ever, Tony Shryane had arranged to be recording Dan and Doris's golden wedding celebrations and that gave most of the cast an excuse to be in the studio that day.

A special solid-gold version of the medallion had been made for Princess Anne and I had been asked to present it to her. It was, of course, a great honour and I was frightened to death of what I should say or, even worse, of becoming tongue-tied. I fretted about it all the time we were waiting for her and I also remembered how my arthritis had let me down when I curtsied to her grandmother. I made a mental note not to bend my knees but just to bob my head.

When she came into the studio, looking

radiant in a beautiful lime-green coat and matching hat, I felt really agitated. The medallion was in a small presentation box and I had been told to hand it to the Princess with the lid open so that she could see immediately what it was. My hands were so stiff and painful that I found it very difficult to get the catch undone. I was red with embarrassment at the thought of presenting a tightly-shut black box instead of a beautiful gold medallion. But just as Tony Shryane introduced me there was a click and the box opened. I almost wept in relief as I thrust it into her hand, and to this day I do not know whether or not I made a proper bow. If I did, my knees must have behaved themselves because I had no problems, and as the Princess smiled and chatted with every bit as much charm as the Queen Mother, my nervousness disappeared. I told her the medallion was to mark our twenty-first anniversary. 'Why that means the programme's as old as me,' she said with great glee, and she told me she had just celebrated her own twenty-first birthday. She said she was delighted to receive such a lovely memento of her visit to Ambridge and that her grandmother, who was one of our regular listeners, would be even more pleased. I got a tremendous thrill from her enthusiastic response and when I congratulated her on becoming 'Horsewoman of the Year' instead of 'Sportswoman of the Year' it did not seem to matter. She was gracious enough not to correct me and just smiled even more widely than before.

It was hard to believe that only a few months earlier I had been down in the dumps, thinking about giving up my involvement with radio. Now here I was, meeting royalty and feeling on top of the world. Arthritis or no arthritis, it was great to be alive and working with The Archers.

CHAPTER FOURTEEN

When we heard on the day of the twenty-first birthday party that there was some kind of row going on between Godfrey Baseley and his new bosses, no one was particularly surprised, nor did any of us give it too much thought. We all knew about Godfrey's aggressive single-mindedness in relationship to The Archers, and there had been many turbulent periods during the long run. We all assumed this was just another one of those occasions and we thanked our lucky stars that we, for once, were not involved.

When he did not turn up for the party—in the new and elegant boardroom at Pebble Mill—we were left with a feeling of unease. A few days later we heard that the row was more serious than any of us imagined and rumours started to fly about—that Godfrey had been sacked and would not be coming back. It was said that he did not like the management's plans for The Archers and that when he had protested, he was given the option of going along with the proposals or of giving up his job.

I did not take the gossip seriously. Although Godfrey was officially over the BBC's retirement age, he was still only a year or so older than me and certainly fitter than many men half his age. It was inconceivable that anyone could sack a man like that who had done so much for the BBC. I thought it was just a matter of time before all the bother was sorted out. But this time it was different and a few days later, he himself announced that he had been sacked.

The BBC promptly denied that they had asked him to leave. He, they said, had not liked the future plans for the programme and had decided to retire.

I have no idea what went on behind the scenes and therefore cannot offer any confirmation of either claim. But the fact remains that Godfrey never did come back and we never got the chance to say farewell. It was all very sad and some of us were quite resentful of the BBC for allowing things to get so out of hand. If we did not feel insulted exactly, we did feel that our egos were badly bruised. We believed that our programme was very important to the BBC, and that therefore the man who had created it deserved better than to be allowed simply to disappear.

No one could deny Godfrey's determination had been the most important factor in getting The Archers off the ground and keeping it going so successfully, nor could there be any question about his total commitment. In his own book, *The Archers: a Slice of My Life*, he wrote:

Never in my wildest hopes or dreams did I anticipate that it was to become, and continue to be, so much an integral part of my own life over all these years and that the characters in this imaginary village of Ambridge would become as real to me as my own family, friends and neighbours, and that I should get to know every field, wood, stream, lane, footpath and building better than I know those in the parish in which I live.

But that is how it is. Perhaps it is not so surprising, since nearly half my adult life has been concerned with collecting, researching and promoting the material that has gone to make up the programme and, even before that, the years of personal experience of living and working in a rural atmosphere and surroundings provided such a wide range of experiences, which all in their own way have played a part in laying down the right kind of foundations on which to build a structure that has proved to be so acceptable to so many people.

Godfrey was a countryman born and bred. He was brought up in a little village in Worcestershire where his father was the local butcher. Godfrey, in his quieter moods, sometimes told us stories about when he left school and worked for his father. His main job was to deliver the meat and that meant plodding around the district in a horse and cart. It was then that he started acquiring his almost encyclopaedic knowledge of country folk and their way of life. I often wondered if he had actually come across a Doris Archer in his travels and if so, how my portrayal matched up to the real farmer's wife. I was never friendly enough with him to ask, and he certainly never volunteered the information. But he was always the fount of knowledge when The Archers was launched and I do not think anyone ever caught him out on anything to do with rural life.

I did not always agree with the way Godfrey handled the running of the programme but I respected his drive and energy and I would be the first to acknowledge just how important he had been to The Archers and therefore to all of us who worked on it.

Apart from all the personal feelings, his going—or more accurately, the way of his going—caused yet another crisis of confidence for many of us. If the programme's very creator could be dispensed with, no one was safe. If this was what being twenty-one, and therefore grown-up, was about, then most of us would have wanted the clock turned back.

The hands of the clock, of course, went in the opposite direction and in time we learnt that Godfrey's disagreement had been over plans to change the writing and editorial control of the programme. The management, having seen the strain on Edward J. Mason and the price he paid for twenty years of lonely responsibility, felt that they could not let anyone else carry such a heavy burden and had decided to recruit a leading dramatist to join the programme and to strengthen the scriptwriting operation. With some justification, Godfrey pointed out that the programme had done quite well enough during the previous years with just himself and two writers. A small team, he felt, meant closer and more coherent relationships and a greater degree of commitment. The bigger groups became, the greater the opportunity for things to fall down the hole in the middle. But the management were adamant that some change was necessary and pointed out that many of the difficult times for the programme could be directly attributed to the health of the writers.

When Godfrey left, there was a longish period when no one seemed to replace him and—to all our surprise—The Archers did not seem to fall to pieces. We were told that the audience figures and the general appreciation of the programme had taken a nasty turn for the worse and this, no doubt, was the real worry that had caused the management to act. The cast were never privy to any of the official audience-research details but we did hear that in answer to one question, something like five times as many listeners said they thought the programme had deteriorated as said it had got better. And, of course, we had our own grapevine—all the people we met during personal appearances. From the remarks coming from that source—the most regular criticism I heard was that we had become too middle-class, more county than country—it did seem as if we were losing our grip. The only saving grace as far as I was concerned was that both official and unofficial sources suggested the acting was still very good. Thus we felt personally exonerated from the criticism and in our artistic arrogance we felt safe in assuming that once the management pulled up their socks and sorted out the script problems, we would be able to win back the affection of our listeners. I think some of us were even quite cheered by the situation because it seemed to underline what we all believed, that the performance of the cast was a major factor in the programme's success.

When Malcolm Lynch replaced Godfrey as script-editor there was undoubtedly a feeling of shock among the cast, not because of anything we knew about him, but mainly because of where he came from: *Coronation Street*. Some of us were horrified that someone from television should be brought in; some that he was from *commercial* television; some that his experience was in such an aggressively urban programme; and all of us, of course, because we were simply frightened of the unknown.

It was probably, therefore, quite a pleasant surprise for some when Malcolm arrived and we discovered he did not have horns. He was a very different kind of man to Godfrey, the big, healthy, loud-spoken countryman. He was small and thin, with one of those faces that you knew had been lived in, and he smoked non-stop. But though he might have spoken quietly, he had very definite views about what he wanted to do with The Archers and quickly stamped his authority on the programme.

From what I gathered from the sidelines, he had been asked to re-examine every aspect of the programme and, if necessary, to do some rebuilding. He set to with a will and we quickly found a new sense of drama in Ambridge with births, deaths and marriages happening at a furious pace and changes taking place at the village shop, the pub, Grey Gables and even at Brookfield Farm. There was a burglary in which Jack Woolley was violently attacked, we got a new vicar and for the first time ever, Doris got tiddly at a wine and cheese evening she had organized.

The BBC bosses described all this as 'a breath of fresh air' but for those of us standing in the draught, it felt more like a howling gale. After years in the comfortable rural backwater, where our various characters had developed a relaxed, low-key attitude to life, we were now fully engaged in a fast-moving drama. June Spencer (who plays Peggy Archer) put it very neatly when she said she was going through the change of scriptwriter in the way that other women went through the change of life.

I think most of us felt unhappy at the developments and from the listeners' comments that I heard, the audience was none too happy either. It was all very unnerving and one or two people actually said that if this was the shape of things to come, they would not really want to be part of it. Up until then The Archers had been a special kind of programme, reflecting a rural life-style that most of the urban listeners had dreams about, helping them forget their own troubles. Now, said those critics, it was just another soap opera. I was too old to have such high principled-views, but I do not think it was exactly the most glorious of times in the programme's long run.

During the most traumatic moments, the management maintained a tight-lipped silence, neither seeking our views nor offering their own. But as the shock waves dispersed a little, Jock Gallagher made more regular appearances in the studio and, in a series of apparently casual remarks, made it clear that the shake-up had been seen as necessary to stop the programme sliding into stagnation. Then we began to get little bits of information about the confidential audience-research reports. Although some listeners felt that all the changes had made the programme less believable, most people found it much less boring, and the decline in numbers listening regularly had not only stopped but had been reversed, though only very slightly.

The one snippet of news that did not please me very much was that although my performance as an actress was still the most highly-rated of all the cast, Doris's 'likeability' had dropped so that she was then only sixth in popularity with listeners. If my performance appreciation had shown a similar decline, I would have worried that my health problems were beginning to show through to my portrayal of Doris and I know I would have realized it was time to give up. But that was not the case and the report made me feel that I was a victim of the scriptwriters' loss of sympathy, presumably because as young men they did not really understand the ways of an elderly lady. Nor did they seem inclined to try. Unlike Ted Mason and Geoffrey Webb, they did not come to talk to us very much and therefore there was little chance of our own personalities now having much impact on our characters. The only one of the writers who did know me well was Norman Painting—his pen name was Bruno Milna—and I always enjoyed doing his scripts best of all. Unfortunately he did not write all that often and I began to get quite worried about losing my place on the centre stage without there being anything that I could personally do to stop that happening.

Once again I toyed with the idea of retiring—always quit while you're on top, they say—but whenever I mentioned it there was always some kind soul, like Tony Shryane, ready to talk me out of it. I was always glad that they did. Without my work, I am quite sure I could have become a really miserable creature, just sitting around feeling sorry for myself. As it was, I was able to carry on meeting all my friends and colleagues regularly and I was also able to use my position as a platform for telling people about arthritis and how one could learn to live with it. I found that very satisfying because I felt I was actually being useful, which in turn gave me more confidence to carry on in The Archers.

The programme, too, regained its old confidence and slowly but surely we settled back into a fairly comfortable routine. We had, I think, found our new place in the broadcasting spectrum. We were no longer at the top of the league as far as numbers were concerned—although we still counted our regular listeners in millions—but we were still regarded with the affectionate familiarity that the British have for their institutions. We were an enduring element of the landscape, very much public property. It was a nice feeling.

As has happened so often over the years, our peace had no sooner descended than it was disturbed. Malcolm Lynch became ill and then seriously ill. Before he had even been with us for a year, he was forced to retire on health grounds.

Again our personal feelings of sympathy for Malcolm were confused with self-concern. Would his going bring about another upheaval? Were we going to be faced with more uncomfortable change? It was some months before we heard what was going to happen, and then there were a few wry comments when we learned that Malcolm was being replaced by two people.

I think what happened was the management had been aware of the problem of Malcolm not having any background or real interest in the countryside, and when they set out to find a new editor, they simply could not find anyone with Godfrey Baseley's breadth. So for script-editor, they settled for a man with a lot of experience in radio and brought in someone else to act as agricultural adviser. The new pair were Charles Lefeaux and Anthony Parkin.

Charles Lefeaux was delightfully theatrical; a lovely little man with a mane of beautiful white hair and a goatee beard to match. He was every inch the ex-actor and had just retired from the radio drama department in London, where he had been one of the most distinguished producers. There were, as you might by now expect, one or two groans about his Hampstead address but he endeared himself to me by declaring himself passionately interested in good food. He was an inspector for one of the famous guides and he used to regale us with stories of some of the wonderful meals he had had around Britain.

Anthony Parkin was the BBC's Agricultural Editor, whom I only knew from listening to his Saturday morning programme, *On Your Farm*. I regarded that as a little bit of homework and I am sure it did help me with my role as Doris. Anthony was himself a farmer and he had a very healthy weatherbeaten look that gave you a lovely feeling of confidence that he could tell you anything there was to know about farming.

Once we had met both of them, most of us relaxed. With their combined experience and their complementary styles, we felt we would not go far wrong. The Archers was in safe hands.

CHAPTER FIFTEEN

One of the big problems for the writers of The Archers has been how to reflect what is going on in the country while at the same time maintaining a strict political balance within the programme. Life became particularly difficult during the long period of debate about the Common Market. I do not pretend to know the ins and outs of it, but I do know it was a major issue for farmers and it was a strong talking point among them for several years before we actually joined in 1973. In Ambridge, however, discussion of the issues was somewhat muted because the writers simply could not find a way of maintaining the political balance.

The difficulty was that, over the years, Dan Archer had become such a realistic character that he was seen by many people as something of an opinion leader. He was also seen as a man with very positive views so, realistically, if he was to be heard talking about the Common Market, he would have made up his mind whether or not he favoured Britain's entry and would be persuading others to his point of view. And, as he was the most influential character in the programme, giving one of the others a contra-stance would not have been seen to be fair to one side or the other. I believe there was some talk of not letting Dan get involved in the debate and leaving it to the other characters, but in the end that was seen to be totally unrealistic and so the whole issue was rather clumsily sidestepped. Even I was aware that we were not living up to our reputation at that time, because everywhere we went around the country people were always very heated in their arguments and I was always conscious of their views. The only thing that happened within the programme was that we did one of our topical inserts on the day of the referendum.

Once Britain actually did join, plans were immediately made for The Archers to catch up on the situation, and we were told that we were going in to the Common Market too, literally: a large group of the cast was to make a promotional trip to Holland. As the storyline justification was that some of the Ambridge farmers should see how Common Market agriculturists went about their business, I assumed that I would not be one of the travellers and, in view of my creaky old joints, I was quite happy to stay at home. But the writers were apprised of the economics of group travel and encouraged to conceive of reasons why some of the womenfolk should make the journey. I found myself very definitely on the list.

Because of my arthritis, I had by now taken on a full-time companion to help me with all the fiddly problems of dressing—buttons, zips and shoelaces were all beyond my thickening fingers—and to my amazement, Tony Shryane said that she could come along with me. I think the BBC did not want the bother of having to look after me!

This was The Archers' first foreign trip—unless you regard Ireland as foreign—and we were all very excited, although that became mingled with apprehension when we learned that we would not be flying, but travelling by coach and ferry. That, however, had its compensations in that there were no real restrictions on the amount of luggage we could take, nor would there by any problems about lugging cases around airports. Once we boarded the coach in Birmingham, we would stay with it until we got back.

We left Pebble Mill on a Saturday morning, complete with a packed lunch, and in the luxury coach normally used by the Aston Villa football team. On this occasion, the club's name was well hidden by the legend 'Ambridge to Amsterdam'.

When we arrived at Hull, I learned for the first time that the crossing of the North Sea would take something like fourteen hours and that we had all been allocated sleeping cabins. My berth was on Deck 'D'. Once on board ship, I discovered to my dismay that 'D' was the lower deck and appeared to be somewhere in the bowels of the ferry. The berths there, I was assured, were the most comfortable of all and I would have plenty of room and so on. Which was all very well, but 'D' Deck could only be reached by clambering down narrow and steep little companionways. On this occasion, 'D' was not for Doris. There was no way I could clamber anywhere.

The purser was marvellous. He grasped the problem instantly, labelled me as not a well lady and sent me to the hospital! The 'hospital' was a cabin on the main deck, distinguished only by the red cross on the door and a high-sided cot instead of a bunk, but it was fine—until I got into bed and said goodnight to my companion. Almost as soon as she had gone to find her berth on 'D' Deck, I decided to go to the loo. I couldn't: the high sides of the cot—they are always used for sick people at sea—were locked in position and my wretched fingers could not undo the catches. It was a very long night and I lay there in agony, listening to the sea slosh all around me! It was a relief in every sense of the word when we got off the boat next morning at the giant Europort at Rotterdam.

Our first real experience of what being in the Common Market might mean came when we stopped at Schipol Airport to meet a couple of journalists and to have a cup of coffee. Admittedly we had our coffee in a fairly posh hotel, but Jock Gallagher went quite white when he went to pay for thirty cups and got a bill for nearly seventy-five pounds. That was just a sign of things to come.

Having been so expensively refreshed, we drove off through the Netherlands—we had learned very quickly that the Dutch did not like the use of the word Holland because that was just one region of the country—up north to Flevoland where we met the Common Market's Dan and Doris, Mr and Mrs De Boer, who had a farm that was reckoned to be similar to Brookfield. They were lovely people who seemed to enjoy entertaining us and showed us around the farm with great pride, explaining how it was on land only recently reclaimed from the sea. And, of course, to our shame they spoke in impeccable English. In fact, when it came to recording a couple of scenes for the programme, I thought Tony Shryane was going to have to ask them to put on a bit of an accent to make them sound foreign.

The next day we went to the studios of Radio Nederland in Hilversum to record some more scenes with Dutch actors, whose accent was also too good for our purposes. It was while we were in Hilversum—a town almost entirely given over to broadcasting in the Netherlands because there are so many different groups and organizations involved—that we discovered that we were listened to regularly by something like 10,000 Dutch people. The times of our broadcasts were even listed in their equivalent of

214

the *Radio Times*.

In between recordings, we also managed to fit in some sight-seeing. We saw Gouda cheese being made (in conditions that did not suggest hygiene was an important factor), we visited one of the biggest permanent agricultural exhibitions in the world (where you can walk round three full-size working farms), we toured Amsterdam (including a visit to the Reijks Museum), witnessed an amazing flower auction (where about three million flowers were sold in about two hours), and looked around the famous Delft pottery factory (where few resisted the temptation to buy a souvenir).

It was evidently a more expensive trip than expected. The Netherlands tourist agency had booked all the hotels for us and I gathered from Jock Gallagher that they had provided more elaborate accommodation than we had asked for. The result was that by the time we headed for our last stop-over point, The Hague, funds were running pretty low. Jock reckoned that he had just about enough money left for our last night's hotel, 'as long as it isn't the Ritz.' It was. Well, not the Ritz, but the Dutch equivalent: the very plush Hotel Bel Air. I will never forget the look on Jock's face as the coach swung into this beautiful park, swept up a very long drive and came to a halt alongside Rolls-Royces, Mercedes and other very expensive cars. A whole host of liveried flunkies descended on us to whisk away our luggage. While we were registering, Jock went around whispering to people to be careful what they ate and drank and he was clearly very embarrassed, unsure as to whether or not he would have enough cash to cover the bill. Just as Tony Shryane was planning a face-saving operation—with a collection of all our personal stocks of guilders— the lady from the tourist board arrived to declare that we were to be the guests of the city council, who would look after all the bills for the night's accommodation and food. You can imagine the relief; maybe the Common Market was not so bad after all!

There were three journalists with us on the trip and the press coverage we got was quite amazing. There was a whole column on the front page of *The Times*—so prominent that none of us noticed it because we expected any small item to be inside the paper—a big story with pictures in the *Daily Express* and a splash in *The Sun*. It was nice to know that our promotional activities were still having some impact and that journalists continued to find us interesting to write about.

The other major piece of promotion we were involved in at that time was yet another issue of the *Borchester Echo*. This one, however, was different from all the previous editions in that it was a total fiction. It was, simply, the *Borchester Echo* and it carried all the little stories that you

216

would find in any local paper: it advertised all the shop-keepers and traders around the Borchester district and even had a classified section that included a house for sale in Ambridge. For once there was no mention of the BBC and no indication that The Archers was just a radio programme. There were, of course, pictures of several members of the cast— including me in what I thought was a stunning lilac head-to-toe outfit—but we were all there as our characters, and reality was not allowed to intrude.

It was very effective and I understood it brought in quite a few inquiries about the house thought to be for sale in Ambridge. That surprised me, because I thought that with the advent of television and with all the fairly dramatic 'progress' that had taken place in Britain, there was little chance for the dreamers to go on believing so strongly in the fiction of The Archers.

From what I could see there had been quite a change in the kind of audience we now had. Originally, when we were at our peak on the Light Programme, just about everybody seemed to listen to us and it was not really all that surprising that some of them should regard us as real people. As television lured many of our listeners away, I thought we were left with an up-market audience—by this time we were going out on Radio Four—who simply enjoyed our bit of gossip and accepted the programme at face value, as a piece of gentle escapism. It is true that we still got a lot of mail addressed to Dan, Doris and company, but these were usually from people who were using our character names because they simply did not know our real names.

The fact that few people knew our names was one of the more frustrating bits about being in The Archers. People who go into the theatre are usually in search of fame, and that usually comes from the recognition of their talents and is symbolized by the name-in-lights accolade. For some reason that I cannot understand, that did not happen to us. We were highly successful by any standards, our performances were constantly praised and everywhere we went we were certainly given star treatment—but always as characters from The Archers, never as actors.

I used to talk to Norman Shelley, one of the great names in radio, and he had the same feeling of frustration. Norman was the actor who created the part of Winnie the Pooh and lots of other lovely children's characters; and appeared in more Shakespearean productions than almost anyone else in the business. By the time he joined The Archers as Colonel Danby, he had already done more than fifty years as a professional and his talent was acknowledged by all his peers, yet few people outside would even know his name.

Norman, who had a wonderful touch of theatrical arrogance in his make-up, used to get quite angry at times, especially when some of our theatre colleagues appeared in the Honours Lists. 'Damn it, the man's never played before more than a couple of hundred sycophantic theatre-goers in his life,' he said, quite bitterly, when one very well known stage actor was given an OBE. And he articulated the feelings of many of us in radio when he said: 'Don't the blighters up there know what we do for the arts? Don't they know that through this wonderful medium (radio) we have given drama to millions of people who would never have thought about going to the theatre? Doesn't that count for anything?'

Well, it did not seem to and we all continued to feel slightly cheated, and it may have been this more than anything else that drove us inwards to our character roles. After all, if Doris Archer was seen as something of a star and no one took a great deal of notice of Gwen Berryman, I would have had to have been superhuman to insist on being myself all the time. (This chapter was written before I knew I was to receive an Honour in the 1981 New Year's List, but it is how I felt at the time and I do not want to alter it because the principle is unchanged.)

The fact that I was not superhuman was constantly underlined for me almost every time

I put my feet on the floor as I got out of bed in the mornings. My joints creaked and the dulling pain ran through me as a reminder that arthritis is a constant companion. It was also a hint that at my age, I ought to be thinking of putting my feet up and taking life easy. Well I did think about it, quite a lot really. In fact, I decided to start winding down gradually and as a first step I chose to move to Torquay, where the weather always seemed a little kinder to my weary bones. Some of my friends thought I was mad to move so far away from the Midlands, where I was brought up and where my career was still centred. Others thought it was the best move I had made in years.

Devon was always very special to me. It was the scene of many of my happiest childhood memories because my parents were very fond of it and they took me and my brother Trevor there for several summer holidays. It was the one place in Britain where I knew the sun shone all the time: it never dawned on me that we only went there in the summer months and that it might, therefore, rain during the other seasons.

I had the added incentive that Trevor and his family had moved to Torquay when he retired from the Wolverhampton business he had inherited from Dad. He had bought a beautiful flat in a lovely new block, right on the sea-front with a magnificent view across the bay. I always envied him the view and when he told me that another flat in the block had come on to the market, I was delighted. When I saw it was on the ground floor—and not a stair in sight—I decided at once to buy it and face the upheaval of leaving the Midlands.

Between buying and moving in, not unnaturally, I had lots of doubts, but these were quickly dispelled by the friendliness of all the neighbours and the sheer joy of breathing good, clean air. I transferred to the local branch of the Soroptimists and therefore immediately found a ready-made group of acquaintances. As Torquay is such a popular holiday centre for Midlanders, I also discovered that my flat was an ideal café for lots of my old friends to drop in for a cup of tea.

Living so close to my brother gave me a nice, comfortable feeling of security and I settled in happily. Instead of dreading the long journeys back to Birmingham, as I had half-expected, I actually looked forward to the regular recording sessions at Pebble Mill. The trip did not take all that long by car—I was still driving myself then—and I always felt refreshed and enthusiastic when I switched from the calm of Torquay to the hustle and bustle of The Archers.

I think the only thing that bothered me then was the way my character was going. For reasons best known to the writers, Doris Archer had become a bit of a nag and was always harassing poor old Dan. I got a bit sick of her constant whining and so did many of the listeners. I got several letters complaining about my lost sense of humour and one woman wrote that if I went on being nasty to Dan, she would not listen any more. It was not the nastiness itself that bothered me—I always preferred the sharper side of Doris to the awful tweeness she sometimes exuded—but I did miss the humour. It was rather ironic looking back on my career, because in my early stage days, when I was playing in comedy, I always wanted straight parts; now when I had the straightest of straight roles, I desperately wanted to make people laugh.

I suppose the truth is that I had lost confidence in the scriptwriters. My loss of points in the opinion poll must have lodged in my subconscious and it was undoubtedly still rankling with me. I did not say anything to anyone about how I was feeling because I was worried about upsetting anyone and I assumed—because no one said otherwise to me—that the rest of the cast was perfectly happy. It must have been old age creeping on, I told myself. But just then we got wind of another audience research report that suggested that the listeners, or at least some of them, were suffering from the same lack of confidence.

We heard some really scathing comments from the report:

Some of the characters are so unpleasant and so wrigglingly embarrassing that one listens with an awful fascination.

Although I'm hooked on it, I find the serial is often trivial and boring with unreal characters.

It isn't interesting and it isn't worth hearing . . . but it's curiously addicitive. I smoke, but I don't commend the habit.

And these were the comments of our friends, the regular listeners!

But the section that underlined my own feelings was the one that said: 'Almost everyone in Ambridge seems abnormally selfish or bitchy and guaranteed to misunderstand everyone else and yet, at the same time, they are evidently meant to be normal and reasonably likeable people.'

Those were indeed the dog days of The Archers, but then the programme had known many difficult times and had always managed to ride the storm. For once, none of us seemed to have any doubt but that we would somehow do so again.

CHAPTER SIXTEEN

One cold, damp day in 1975, I did the most extraordinary thing: I told the BBC that I was ready to die!

If that makes me seem slightly demented, it is probably because I was at the time, by my old enemy, arthritis. Lulled by the pleasures of living in Torquay, I had pushed my aches and pains into the background and journeyed to and from Birmingham whenever I was wanted in the studio. But suddenly that terrible feeling of broken glass being pushed into my knees came back and every trip became more agonizing than the previous one. I needed more and more frequent visits to my doctor and more and more time to rest. I had to cut down on my appearances in the programme and I had to think hard about the future—for me and for Doris.

I still did not want anyone else to take over the part and it had finally dawned on me that if the programme was to go on, the only solution for the writers would be for Doris Archer to die.

I knew what that would do for me. I knew how shattering it would be to my morale. I was fully aware how much Doris had been part of my life and that, as I have already admitted, she had sometimes seemed my whole life. I could also guess at what it would do to many of the listeners—how, if all those letters were anything to go by, many of the lonely people would feel they had lost a close friend. It was that as much as anything else that made the decision so difficult.

On the other hand, my arthritis was causing so much trouble that I felt I had no option. I told Tony Shryane that I wanted to leave and that I was quite prepared to do the death scene before I went. He was quite shaken, but he knew me very well and obviously accepted that I was not acting without having given it a lot of thought, so he did not say very much. But within minutes the heavy mob arrived, in the shape of Jock Gallagher, whose title I never knew but who was one of the radio bosses at Pebble Mill. He too was shaken by my intention, but unlike Tony Shryane, he had a lot to say. He told me how much the BBC appreciated my long service and my major contribution to the success of The Archers. He acknowledged his promise not to re-cast the part of Doris. It was unthinkable, he said. I had made the character so much my own that it would not be fair to ask anyone else to try to follow my performance. 'There can never be another Doris Archer,' he added, 'and if you do decide to retire, then we will, of course, work out how best to handle it in the script.'

I was suddenly aware of his use of the word *if*.

When we had started the conversation, I had not thought there was any *if* about it. I had made up my mind and knew exactly what I was going to do. Now it did not seem like a decision any more, only a possibility. As soon as I saw it as a *possibility*, it hit me that it was one that I did not like one little bit. My resolution wavered. I had made a mistake and here was this nice young man offering me a chance to put things right. He said he realized that I could not go on travelling so often, but what about cutting down on the number of trips? What about just coming up occasionally? And if he could help with transport, he would be only too pleased. The more he talked, the less sure I became and in the end I said I would stay on for at least another few months.

But that did not take away my arthritis, so we worked out an arrangement with Tony Shryane whereby I reduced my travelling to once a month. As long as I was heard on the air regularly, he said, the listeners would not mind much the gaps between my appearances. 'They'll think you've just popped out to do the shopping or visit Mrs P or something like that,' he said.

It turned out to be a very good compromise. Although I had undoubtedly been sweet-talked into carrying on. I was nevertheless delighted at not having to sever my connection with the programme altogether.

I thought I might get fed-up with the month-long gaps, but I didn't. They were just about right. However, I suspect that was only because I had, in any case been feeling less involved not only with the programme but also with some of the cast. Over the years there had been huge changes in The Archers. Writers and editors had come and gone, and the number of actors and actresses who had passed through was enormous. Of the originals, only Tony Shryane on the production side and June Spencer, Norman Painting and myself were left. The big-family feeling that we once enjoyed so much was no longer there. With all the changes, there were so many new characters that I never really got to know any of them very well. Before, we really did seem like relatives to each other, and to me it seemed a pity that we had lost that feeling. I had enjoyed being a matriarchal figure! There was nothing really wrong, of course. It was just that The Archers had necessarily changed to suit the times and I had been rather left behind in the process. I think it is something that happens to most old folk. I did not feel bitter about it, as I gather many of my generation do. Indeed, I was delighted about one of the new developments—the growing appeal the programme seemed to have for young people. I had noticed that the journalists who came to write about us were getting younger all the time, but I put that down to my own advancing years and the policemen-are-getting-younger syndrome. But it was always those younger ones—and especially girls with university degrees—who knew most about the programme from their own listening. And then another audience-research report indicated that we had a 'lower age profile' than for Radio Four in general. That was interpreted for me as meaning more younger listeners tuned in specially to The Archers, and that was obviously a very healthy sign. It indicated that there was still some future for the programme and I was glad still to be a part of it.

An article in one of the colour supplements picked up that optimism with the lovely headline 'Forever Ambridge' (which Norman Painting later used as the title for his book) and forecast: 'The soap opera is unlikely to be outmoded; in one form or another it will always be with us.'

We were by now heading towards another anniversary—our twenty-fifth, an amazing quarter of a century—and, as before, there was another flurry of press interest in the months leading up to it. In a two-page feature, the *Sun* described us as 'The Astonishing Archers' and, after recounting how the programme began, went on to give an up-to-date assessment:

Times have changed. And The Archers have tried to change with them. In 1951, Dan's big

228

decision was to pension off his two workhorses, Boxer and Blossom, and invest in a tractor.

Down the years, developments in farming have been faithfully followed up at Brookfield. Attitudes have altered too. In that first year, producer Tony Shryane passed a script in which Dan refused a cup of tea from Doris before going on a coach trip. 'You know how I am after a cup of tea,' he said.

Shryane's superiors were deeply shocked. They told him: 'We don't want that sort of stuff in The Archers.'

They got a lot more than that in time, particularly as Dan's grandchildren, Tony and Jennifer, grew up. In 1967, Jennifer had an illegitimate baby. The Archers had joined the permissive society.

There were also photographs of all the main characters and details of how we had started off earning about £10 a week but were then on about £5,000 a year. But I was quoted—accurately, for once—as saying that the programme had given me something much more valuable than a good salary: it had kept me young in mind, and very happy.

I was also pleased to see in print for the first time the promise that there would never be another Doris.

It wasn't just the press that was interested in looking at The Archers. BBC television had sent in one of their leading documentary producers, Roger Mills, and he made a programme called *Underneath The Archers* that was shown on BBC 2 on the actual day of our twenty-fifth anniversary, 1 January, 1976. (It proved so popular with viewers that it was later repeated.)

Roger had spent several months following various strands of the programme but my involvement was quite small. I was filmed with other members of the cast, recording in the studio, and then the cameras came to my flat in Torquay. I was interviewed at some length, but in the end only two or three minutes of the conversation were seen on the television. The bit they kept in was where I was reminiscing about my one distinction from the rest of the cast: I was the only one actually younger in life than my character. Doris was then seventy-five but I just had my sixty-ninth birthday.

I do not think many of us had ever really noticed or thought much about the connections between our anniversaries and New Year's Day, but being a Scot, Jock Gallagher latched on to it for our Silver Jubilee and our celebrations took the form of a Hogmanay Party.

In the presence of the BBC's Director-General, Sir Charles Curran, and Lady Curran, we started off with a fairly sedate dinner on New Year's Eve. This was at Pebble Mill, where the studio had been beautifully decorated in shimmering silver. At the stroke of midnight, as the bells rang out the old year, all hell seemed to break loose. Twenty-five champagne corks were popped in military-style salute; someone brought in a piper, who played some rousing Scottish tunes; and there were spontaneous cheers all around us. The timing was perfect and we all raised our glasses to toast twenty-five glorious years. The drama of the occasion left hardly a dry eye in the house, or at least that was how it looked to me, through my own tear-filled eyes.

There was an enormous cake—which Lady Curran and I were invited to cut—and some of the cast did some party pieces. The 'cabaret' ended with everyone singing, to the programme's signature tune, a song that was specially written for the occasion:

This is the land we think is grand,
We are the brand of Ambridge.
Once on the soil we used to toil
But things are changing now.
We'd milk a cow, and harness the plough
But it's mechanization with all its row,
The top o' the pops is played to a sow
To bring her to the boil.
A battery hen never knows quite when
It should lay an egg again and again
And even corn is bread when its born
Because of the battery men.

Doris and Dan have got a plan
To live a sweet life in Ambridge;
Whenever there's work they want to shirk,
They leave it all to Phil.
To keep himself sane and use his brain
To work on the farm in sun and rain
Making sure the business shows a gain,
And cows don't go on the pill.
Even cows' moos have turned to boos
Because they've no handsome bull to choose
And the poor old bull finds life so dull
It's developed the AI blues.

Gamekeeper Tom bangs like a bomb
At Woolley's ideas for Ambridge,
'Twas only a bird that once was heard,
But now his peace is attacked.
He used to rear the pheasants each year,
But Woolley now hopes to cross, we fear
A railway engine with a deer
So they can be easily tracked.
Polly, Nora and Sid are making a bid
To make the Bull pay as well as it did
Ten pints a minute were once ordered in it
When Walter was but a kid.

It was a wonderful night and I was so pleased
that I was still there to be part of all the
excitement. I was glad that I had been dissuaded
from retiring. Someone had produced a little
commemorative card which had a space for

autographs, and as I went round collecting signatures and chatting to all the people to whom I had grown so close over the years, I realized how near I had been to giving up the very career that meant almost everything in the world to me. And when I turned over that same card and read the summary of press comments, I also realized just how important The Archers was in the history of broadcasting. The comments are worth listing:

The Archers: happy families—*Liverpool Echo*
It could go on forever—*Birmingham Evening Mail*
It's become a religion—*Daily Mail*
A silver landmark—*Evening Standard*
They aim to run forever—*Liverpool Daily Post*
The world's longest-running soap opera—*Guardian*
Ambridge has moved with the times—*Portsmouth News*
Amusement and entertainment for millions—*Daily Mirror*
The Archers are here to stay—*Express and Star*
25 years of Ambridge life—*Sunday Herald*
A radio heart of England—*Western Daily Press*
Compulsive listening—*Worcester Evening News*
A success by being sincere—*Northern Echo*
Part of Britain's history—*Sunday Sun*
In Ambridge all things are possible—*South Wales Echo*

That night I was able to forget all my pain and anxiety and wallow in self-congratulation. A few weeks later I found myself once again in the middle of a celebration, only this time I really was caught on the hop, by Eamonn Andrews for his *This Is Your Life* programme on commercial television.

Whenever I had seen the programme as an ordinary viewer, I always thought the 'victims' must have had some inkling of what was going on. Either that or they must be daft. But when it happened to me, I can honestly say I did not have a clue. The collusion between Thames Television, who make the programme, and the BBC was total and none of my family or friends breathed a word of the plans that they had obviously been party to.

In fact, the whole thing nearly did not happen, because my arthritis was playing me up and I was in a particularly grumpy mood. We were recording in Birmingham when Tony Shryane said he wanted me to go to Broadcasting House in London the next day for some filming for a Canadian television station. It was not one of the days I was contracted for and I actually had an appointment fixed with my hairdresser back in Torquay. My hair had been a problem for many years because of the psoriasis, and regular hairdressing was very important to me psychologically. I felt really cross about having to miss the appointment and I know I grumbled a great deal about the lack of notice and why on earth I should have to put myself out for the Canadians.

I told Tony that I was much too tired and that I just wanted to go home, but for once he did not seem very sympathetic and more or less insisted that I went, otherwise it would look very unprofessional, he said. I was a bit shocked and reluctantly agreed. I grumbled all the way to London and I am sure everyone must have been thoroughly fed up with me by the time we got into the studio, but that did not stop me complaining about having to work in unfamiliar surroundings. Why on earth could the cameras not have been brought to Pebble Mill, where we could have been filmed in our natural habitat?

There was an awful lot of messing about with lights and microphones, and I was feeling just about ready to explode when the tall, handsome figure of Eamonn Andrews appeared from behind a screen and in that beautiful Irish brogue said: 'Gwen Berryman ... this is your life.'

What happened after that is very hazy. I am sure I cried a lot. I always do when I am happy. I remember everyone at the television studios fussing around me offering champagne all the time, when all I wanted was a nice cup of tea. They had also had one of my evening dresses brought up from Torquay but, probably still smarting from the suggestion that I might have been unprofessional, I had a little fit of artistic temperament and insisted that for continuity reasons I should wear the same dress as when I had been first filmed in the morning.

There was quite a long delay from the time Eamonn introduced himself until we went into the studio to record the programme and by then I was almost frightened about what would happen and who would be brought on to illustrate my life story. But once the lights went on and the audience applauded, I relaxed and felt in my element, once again the centre of attraction. It was lovely and I got thrill after thrill as friends I had not seen for years, friends I had seen only days before, my brother and his family, and finally the whole cast of The Archers came on to the set and said such lovely things about me. It really was an incredible feeling and if the viewers get even a fraction of the enjoyment out of watching the programme that I can now say the 'victim' gets from being in it, there is no wonder it is one of the most popular shows on television. That famous red book—which, incidentally, contains even photographs taken in the studio—and a lovely note from Eamonn are now among my most treasured souvenirs.

If I thought that was the end of the celebrations and the tributes stemming from the

Silver Jubilee. I was wrong. Only a couple of months later, I discovered that I had been named 'Midlander of the Year'.

This is an award to the person who has 'done most in the preceding year to increase the prestige of the Midlands or who has made an outstanding contribution to the social, political, industrial or cultural life of the area'. I felt honoured not just in winning but in being the first woman to do so. In fact the title of the award in previous years had been 'Midland Man of the Year', and winners had included the eminent doctor who had pioneered fertility drugs, the man who had steered through to completion the great National Exhibition Centre and 'the citizens of Birmingham' for the way they responded to the IRA pub bombing in which twenty-two people died. I could not believe that I was entitled to join such a distinguished roll of honour but, of course, I was delighted that other people should think I was worthy of the title.

The award itself took the form of a beautiful silver tea service and a cheque for five hundred guineas (I was really pleased that it was in good, old-fashioned, non-decimal currency). But as if that were not enough, the presentation was made at a splendid banquet at one of Birmingham's finest restaurants, The Plough and Harrow, and there were lots of speeches—mostly about me!

Sir Derek Capper, the Chief Constable of Birmingham and Chairman of the selection panel, said the award was in recognition of the way in which I had 'made a Midland life-style the envy of millions around the world'. Then he spoke about my arthritis and the problems it created, how I had sometimes recorded from my sick-bed: 'For most people that would be enough, but instead of retiring she carried on and even added to her problems by doing charity work on behalf of other arthritis sufferers.'

While I was still blushing, Fred Peart, then Minister of Argriculture and now Lord Peart, got to his feet to make the presentation and to add yet another tribute. He said he wanted to praise me for doing so much for agriculture over the previous twenty-five years, and when he saw me looking puzzled—I had never thought of having done anything for agriculture—he explained that I had helped by depicting so successfully the ups and downs of the farmer's life: 'The warm way of life of Doris and her friends has contributed significantly to an industry which produces half the food we eat and two thirds of the food which is grown commercially.'

That, of course, was precisely what Godfrey Baseley had set out to achieve all those years ago and I was aware that the Minister's comments were a wonderful tribute to Godfrey and all those responsible for the programme. But I was very happy to be the focal point at this particular moment.

When it was time for me to speak, I was very nervous and so, as I often did in such circumstances, I hid behind Doris Archer and explained how difficult it was for a country bumpkin to make a speech to so many distinguished and sophisticated people. It helped to stop my knees knocking!

There was a great deal of press coverage of the award and, for me, one article—in my old local paper, the *Wolverhampton Express and Star*—summed the occasion up perfectly:

Doris Archer in a custodian of rural virtues, the kindly farmer's wife who never lets the scones burn and insists on the jam being home-made.

Not surprisingly, Gwen Berryman ... shares this outlook on life. She radiates old-world values and abhors violence in entertainment, turns off television whenever nudes appear and proclaims the simple virtues personified by The Archers.

But the award is in the name of Gwen Berryman, not Doris Archer. The two interact on the radio, but are not interrelated on a personal level. An actress playing the same part for quarter of a century might become so closely identified with the character as to lose individuality.

Gwen has never allowed overlapping to take control. She has remained the gifted professional radio actress, coming fresh to the part in every episode.

I could not ask for a better critique of my career and to see such remarks in black and white certainly made all the struggle against adversity more than worthwhile.

CHAPTER SEVENTEEN

The euphoria of anniversaries and awards and celebrations wore off all too quickly and by the end of 1976 I had been firmly dragged down to earth again by my now-worsening arthritis—and the approach of my seventieth birthday.

Although I was still managing to drive myself between Torquay and Birmingham every month, I was finding the journey more and more exhausting. I usually travelled up to the studio on the Sunday (for recordings on Monday, Tuesday and Wednesday), and by the time I arrived, I could barely manage to get a bite to eat before collapsing into bed. Getting around Pebble Mill was also very tiring and I spent more and more time in a wheelchair. At home, I was able to live alone but I had to have the district nurse come to see me at least once a week.

Sometimes I just do not know how I managed to keep going. Edgar Harrison said it was because I had such a good sense of humour. He may have been right, but when the pain in my legs and hands was at its height, I can assure you I could not see the funny side of anything. Yet, I was aware that I was an awful lot luckier than most people and certainly much better off than lots of other arthritis-sufferers. I had lots of friends and my brother and his wife were just two floors away in the same block of flats.

In the end the pain got the better of me, and I had to go into the special orthopaedic hospital at Oswestry for a long rest and physiotherapy treatment. I spent my seventieth birthday lying flat on my back!

While I was away from The Archers, it was decided to write Dan out of the script too for a couple of months and to experiment in pushing some of the younger characters towards centre stage. Dan and Doris had dominated the programme right from the beginning, but realistically they could not go on like that much longer. Dan was eighty and Doris was seventy-six.

One of the problems for the writers was that they had never been able to assess the impact of the younger actors and actresses on the listeners and they therefore did not know in which direction they should develop the next generation. They did not even know if there was any point in considering a future without the Grand Old Couple.

Edgar Harrison was not very happy about the experiment and I felt a bit guilty that it had been my illness that precipitated the situation which left Edgar without an appearance for two months. It did not help matters very much when an anonymous BBC spokesman told the press: 'There was no significant audience reaction to the absence of Dan and Doris.' It sounded as if we had not been missed and obviously raised questions about our immediate future.

As always, it was Tony Shryane who was there to pour oil on troubled waters. He told Edgar and me that we were definitely wanted back. He said that the two months had been used for a careful sounding-out process to see what should be the long-term future of the programme, and that it was now clear that lots of younger people were listening and that they would accept the subsequent generations. While that was very healthy for the future, there was no intention of mortgaging the present by getting rid of Dan and Doris.

I was very pleased because the treatment at Oswestry had given me a great deal of relief from pain—enough to enjoy a belated birthday party, which I shared with Edgar, who was also seventy—and I did not feel a bit like retiring. I could even walk up and down stairs again and I really felt on top of the world. So much so that I cheerfully accepted another series of bookings for personal appearances and talks in connection with the arthritis charity organizations. I became so busy that it was sometimes difficult to fit it all in.

People always used to ask me just how I managed to keep going so actively when, by rights, I should have been resting and taking life easy in these twilight years. But I have no secret, unless it was in my refusal ever to give in. I suppose that must represent some strength of character and if it does, I know exactly where I got it from: my father. His courage and determination against much greater odds than I ever faced were there as a constant example. I hope he would have been proud at my efforts to follow him.

Although I was still fully committed to The Archers, I was nowhere near as involved as I had been and I found that slowly but surely my part was becoming less and less important. Obviously it was not easy for the writers to cope with my irregular appearances and with the fact that Doris Archer was creeping towards eighty. They were in something of a straitjacket but I do not think they needed to make Doris seem quite so silly. I seldom had any proper conversation in the script. I just asked the sort of who, what, why, when questions and never really responded on the occasion that they got an answer.

I did, of course, think once again about retiring but by now I was almost scared to mention it. I knew everybody would try to persuade me to stay just a little longer. I think some of them—especially those in the cast—saw me as something of a talisman and they thought that if I left, the programme might fold up. If I had rationalized that, I would have been able to say it was nonsense and I could have pointed to Tony Shryane's assertion that there was now a healthy number of younger listeners who would not miss me when I had gone. But I did not rationalize—probably because I did not want to—and I carried on.

When Tony Shryane retired—in February, 1979—you have no idea how much more tiresome the journey from Torquay to Birmingham became. It was very difficult to accept that Tony would no longer be in charge. He was only sixty—the BBC's normal retirement age—and still with as much energy and enthusiasm as ever. But more important than that, he had been my direct link with the programme for all of the twenty-eight years it had then been running. He had sheltered me from the more tempestuous outbursts of Godfrey Baseley; calmed my shattered nerves on countless occasions; rearranged recording schedules whenever I had the slightest problem; and, most difficult of all, he had directed me with endless patience. It was through him that I had become Doris Archer.

I do not know if British Rail was part of the conspiracy, but I found the trains getting more and more awkward for someone in my condition. All the seats had those little tables in between them, and while I found them quite useful during the journey, they presented me with the dickens of a problem to get out from under them. Nor was it much easier driving. I had caught my hand in the funny handle on the fire door at the hotel I stayed at in Birmingham, and that made my hand and arm even more useless. That meant when I drove up it took me two days, because my hands got so tired trying to grip the steering wheel that I had to stop off half-way at a guest house.

While Tony Shryane was there, I always knew that, whatever happened, he would sort things out when I eventually got to the studio at Pebble Mill. That should not be seen as any reflection on William Smethurst, the new producer of The Archers. It was just that over the years, Tony's help and kindness had been so total that I had developed a high degree of dependence. He had become a kind of security blanket. And, of course, as happens when you remove any kind of blanket, there was an instant loss of warmth.

Fellow-sufferers will know what the cold does to arthritic joints: it makes them so painful you could scream. I wanted to do just that, and if I translated that into reality, it would have meant giving up The Archers. But then I realized I was trapped in a vicious circle. With my loss of security, I needed to be involved with the programme more than ever, but the more I looked at the changes and the diminishing importance of my role, the more I became aware of how insecure my involvement was. But that way lies madness and even if Doris were already in the one created by the writers, I was not ready for any straitjacket. I pulled myself together and decided to carry on trying to beat the odds.

William Smethurst and his various assistants were all very helpful. Whenever I was in the studio, there was always a swivel chair that allowed me to turn around without moving my neck or my spine. It had wheels on it and I was able to 'walk' myself around the different microphone positions, and the microphones themselves were specially-angled to save me straining towards them. I do not know what it must have looked like sometimes, but I was ever so glad we were not on television. If we had been, viewers might have thought they were watching the wheelchair olympics for geriatrics, rather than a soap opera!

I am not sure what effect all this had on my performance because the production staff were endlessly patient. They never criticized anything I did and I know that even if there had been mistakes, they would have used all their technical expertise to sort them out before the listeners heard the programme. But I think I must have been on automatic pilot some of the time. There were moments when I felt my voice threatening to collapse into a pathetic croak but then when the red recording-light went on, my nerves were somehow controlled and I was able to rise to the occasion.

There were, however, no two ways about it. I was not getting any younger and each month seemed to bring more worry and anxiety as I felt myself becoming a little bit more of a cripple. Just to crown it all, I had a diabetes flare-up, and having to watch everything I ate made me feel more frustrated than ever. Those people around me then must have qualified for sainthood because of their patience, understanding and actual help.

At home, when I had difficulty even in washing and dressing, a nurse came to the flat every day to help me. My brother, his family and my local friends were constantly having to do things for me, from posting letters to making meals. I am ashamed to say that sometimes they did not get the gratitude they deserved because I was feeling so awful and, as a result, very self-centred. Instead of thanking them, I griped at just about everything under the sun. I thought about my now-lifeless hand and complained about hotels that did not give enough thought to their disabled guests; I dropped my lunch into my lap and moaned that no one made a tray without a front lip that would enable somebody with my kind of useless hands to slide things on and off; I tried to go to the loo and whined about the lack of handicapped people's facilities. In fact, there was not a great deal that I did not go on about at one time or another. My sense of humour was obviously thinning with my blood.

At work, I had to have all the special arrangements I have already mentioned, and someone always fetched me tea and helped me sort out my lunch arrangements. Instead of being the matriarchal figure able to solve everyone else's worries, I was reduced to dependency on anyone prepared to lend a hand. Again, I am ashamed to say, I took it a bit too much for granted that there always was someone ready to help. I was too often on the 'take' side of the give-and-take relationship that exists among friends.

No one at the BBC suggested that I should think about retiring, but I suspect one or two people were quite relieved when I asked to cut down even further on my recording sessions. It must have been especially difficult for the new, young people involved with the programme to cope with me. In my more maudlin moments I used to think they would see me as a broken down old has-been who still thought she was a star; an ageing actress afraid to give up. I would not have blamed them if they had, but somehow I do not think they did. They treated me with too much genuine affection for that to have been the case.

And it was that affection that made me want to stay on as long as possible. It was nothing to do with being an actress. I knew I was not famous any more, that the clock was much too far on for me to play the leading-lady again. It was not the applause of an appreciative audience I wanted. It was to be happy in the bosom of a large family. I regret very much that fate did not see fit to let me marry and raise my own family. I would have loved children and grand-children of my own and I know that I have missed out on all that. Is it any wonder that I should want to cling to my surrogate family— The Archers—complete with husband, children, grandchildren and even great-grandchildren? What was a little bit of pain in return for all that?

In the end, it was not the pain or the arthritis that stopped me. It was that wretched stroke that left me without any means to battle on. Quarter of a century earlier I had seen my father cut down by the same kind of sudden blow. Even he, a giant of a personality, could find no way back to normal life. I sadly, but quietly, gave up. I accepted that this time it was a final curtain.

CHAPTER EIGHTEEN

Having acted out the final scene and accepted that the play was over, I was really very, very low. I felt almost unbearably sorry for myself and I thought I could feel my spirit ebbing away. At that particular time, I think even death would not have been unwelcome. All that lay ahead was a grim existence, far from the excitements of being a successful actress. But just when the blackness threatened to engulf me completely, I suddenly rediscovered one of the nicest of all the theatrical traditions; that moment of magic for both artiste and audience when a fine performance is rewarded by deliriously-appreciative applause—the curtain call.

I could not quite believe it because it was so unexpected. I had taken a little bow when there was that flurry of interest in my retirement from The Archers, but now here I was being invited to step forward into the spotlight once again, and this time by Her Majesty the Queen.

When they told me that I was to receive the MBE in the New Year's Honours List, I honestly thought I was dreaming. I have already explained just how confused my illness had left me, and I could only think this was still part of it.

As the truth slowly sank in and I realized that I was to become Gwen Berryman, MBE, I was thrilled beyond measure. I felt so proud I could have burst. I am quite sure I would have been very excited by such an honour at any time in my career, but to receive it at the end—when not only had the curtain come down but the lights had started to go out as well—was just incredible. It really was the most wonderful curtain call anyone could have asked for. Not even the best-paid claque in all Italy could have engineered such a moment of glorious rapture!

The feeling lasted for days and it was so difficult not to tell anyone else about it, but I knew it must remain a secret until the Honours List was published. Instead, I began planning—what I should wear, how I would get to the Palace, what I would say to the Queen. It was, once more, great to be alive. And when the announcement was finally made, all the letters and cards poured in with congratulations and good wishes not just from friends and colleagues, but also from listeners, reassuring me that I had not been forgotten.

Slowly, however, the euphoria wore off and realism set in. In my state of health—suffering from arthritis, diabetes and the effects of two crippling strokes—there was really little likelihood of me being able to make the long journey from Torquay to London. I did so much want to meet the Queen and it would have been lovely to see her in her natural surroundings in Buckingham Palace, but I accepted the odds against me were too great. Of course, I was obviously disappointed with that realism, but I consoled myself with the thought of receiving the award in the post and being able to show it off to all my friends when they visited me. I also quietly cherished the hope that the Queen might actually sign the accompanying note herself. A letter with that famous 'Elizabeth R' signature would make a marvellous endpiece to my scrap-book.

In one way, I was quite relieved about not going to the Palace because my speech was still an aggravating problem. When I started a conversation, everything was fine for about five minutes, and then the words just would not come out the way I wanted them to. It could have been quite embarrassing if that happened when I was talking to the Queen. I also had some small consolation in that I had often shared Tony Shryane's memories of his visit to Buckingham Palace in 1961 when he collected his MBE; and those of Norman Painting, who was made an OBE in 1976.

What I did not know, however, was that my brother—well aware of how much I had wanted to go to Buckingham Palace—had actually been investigating all the possibilities of getting me to London in one piece. When he came to see me one day, he told me that it looked as if all the practical problems could be resolved and it was really up to me whether or not I would risk my health and make the journey. There was never a moment's doubt for me. I *would* go to the Palace. I was so thrilled that it was like hearing about the Honour all over again!

Trevor had made arrangements with the Red Cross that they would provide an ambulance to take me to London; and with the nursing home that one of my favourite nurses, Sister Bernice Woodward, would travel with me to look after me. He had also spoke to someone at Buckingham Palace and they had agreed that I would be able to stay in a wheelchair throughout the investiture ceremony.

The day before the ceremony, I was up early and supervised the packing of the wardrobe I had planned for the occasion. When the ambulance arrived, I discovered it was brand new and I was to be the first passenger. It looked very smart in its Red Cross livery and inside it was every bit as comfortable as any limousine. As we pulled away from the nursing home in Torquay, I felt that I was going to London in real style.

Because the ambulance was so new, we drove along fairly steadily and the two-hundred-mile journey took us about seven hours. By the time I arrived at the London hotel, where Trevor and my nephew, Christopher, were waiting for me, I was very tired. But to an actress, the prospect of a public performance is a great reviver, and after a little lie down I felt better and went down to join them for dinner.

I slept like a log that night but as the dawn of the great day broke, I was awake and full of anticipation. Sister Woodward came to help me dress and ordered breakfast for me in the room, only to discover that the hotel's room service was limited to continental breakfast. With what I knew would be an exhausting day before me, I was aware that I really needed a good, solid English breakfast under my belt. I decided to play the temperamental actress and I kicked up a bit of a fuss. It worked, and I got my bacon and eggs.

We were due at the Palace at ten-thirty am with the investiture starting at eleven, but I was so excited and anxious to be there on time that I was ready to go by just after nine o'clock. As we sat around waiting, I think my nervousness must have communicated itself to the others and in the end we set off for Buckingham Palace much too early.

It was a lovely spring-like morning—not what one would expect for early February—and the crowds were out as the ambulance took us down through Piccadilly Circus, along Haymarket to Trafalgar Square, under Admiralty Arch into The Mall. We knew it was still some time before we could go into the palace yard so we were happy to give precedence to most of the other traffic and we just soaked up the atmosphere.

There were lots of spectators milling around the palace gates, and although I knew most of them would be tourists hoping to catch a glimpse of some of the Royal Family, I felt that they were there to be my audience and that the air of suppressed excitement was quite like that in the theatre just before the curtain goes up. It was a lovely feeling.

At long last, the moment came and we drove grandly up to the vehicle entrance to Buckingham Palace and, after a check of our pass, we were waved through.

I felt a bit like a sack of potatoes as they lifted me out of the ambulance and into my wheelchair. I was so excited and anxious not to crease my dress or dislodge my hat that I am sure it must have been very difficult for Sister Woodward and the Red Cross people. But they were wonderful and I felt quite presentable by the time a very smart young army officer came and said he would be looking after me for the whole time I would be in the Palace. I do not know what regiment he belonged to, but my brother said the medal he was wearing was the Military Cross and he immediately became even more of a hero to me.

He took charge of the wheelchair and escorted me, Trevor and Christopher through a private entrance into the Palace. I was pushed into a lift, and was amazed to see how old and rickety it

255

was. We went up one floor and, as we came out of the lift and along a wide corridor, I saw a row of lovely miniatures, which turned out to be portraits of all the Queen's predecessors right back to Henry VIII.

When we arrived at the state ballroom where the investiture ceremony was to take place, I was separated from Trevor and Christopher and the young equerry took me to join the other people who were to receive Honours. I think there were about two hundred of us altogether and as we sat waiting, an orchestra—in a minstrels' gallery high above us—played various selections of very lively music. When they started on tunes from 'The Desert Song' I felt like joining in and singing. It would have been the perfect setting for a performance but, realizing that discretion was the better part of valour and knowing all too well that my once-fine voice was now like a corncrake, I restrained myself and contented myself with looking around and trying to spot the well-known faces. I think I recognized several politicians, but apart from Angus Maude, I could not put names to them. I did see television personality Robin Day, and Arthur Askey, but I did not notice Anton Dolin, the famous dancer, until he came over to talk to me and we exchanged congratulations. It was wonderful to be acknowledged by such a professional.

I was also thrilled to receive a special message

of good wishes from the bandsmen of the Scots Guards, who had been playing the music outside the Palace. I was staggered that they should even know who I was because they were all so young, but one of the officers told me later that when they were serving abroad, The Archers— which they heard on the British Forces Broadcasting Service—was one of their most important links with home. 'The programme still represents much of what's best about Great Britain, and don't forget most of these lads are in uniform because they are so fiercely patriotic,' he told me. It was that simple message from those young soldiers that, more than anything else, made me feel I might just have done something after all to merit the great honour that was about to be bestowed on me by the Queen. I swelled unashamedly with pride at their spontaneous acknowledgement.

As a clock somewhere in the distance began to strike the hour, the door of the ballroom was thrown open and the royal party swept in. Leading the way were the Beefeaters—the Captain and four Yeomen of the Guard, resplendent in their stunning scarlet tunics, with the gold embroidered crown and royal cypher, knee breeches, flat velvet hats and ruffs. They all carried the ceremonial halberds and had swords slung from broad leather belts. For me, the Beefeaters symbolized the traditions of the British monarchy and, knowing that they only turn out for very special occasions, I had a great thrill of being, even if only for a moment, a part of history.

Behind the Beefeaters came another guard party from the armed services in modern uniform, and then Her Majesty, Queen Elizabeth. We all held our breath as she went to her place on a little platform at the front of the ballroom, flanked by the Beefeaters and her various aides and officials. As the band played the national anthem, I was the only one not standing rigidly to attention. I could not get up from my wheelchair, but I promise you my salute was inside me and was as passionately loyal as any of those who could show it in the traditional manner.

The ceremony began with the Home Secretary, Mr Whitelaw, reading out the citations for those receiving their awards for political services, and each one moved forward to be presented to the Queen. Those who were being knighted actually did kneel before her, and she touched them on both shoulders with an enormous sword that looked very heavy. I know all the storybooks tell us that that is how knights are knighted, but I was still very surprised.

When the political honours had been distributed, Mr Whitelaw disappeared and the Lord Chamberlain then read out the citations for the rest of us, in strict order of rank, and alphabetically for those who were equal.

I was so fascinated by all that was going on that I did not realize that it was my turn next, until the young equerry whispered in my ear and I felt my wheelchair being propelled towards the Queen. My heart was pounding and, in terror, I realized that there was no way I could get up on to the little platform as everyone else had done. I felt awful. Here I was, despite all the odds, actually before Her Majesty and just about to embarrass everyone by not being able to rise to the occasion. But that was only because I did not, at that moment, fully appreciate how carefully such occasions are planned.

As my wheelchair came to a halt in front of her, the Queen immediately stepped off the platform and bent over to hand me the MBE, smiled radiantly and thanked me for all the pleasure I had given so many people over so many years. I was so taken aback by the swiftness of her reaction that all I could say in return was that I felt honoured and privileged to meet her. I wanted to hold the centre stage as long as possible and I wanted to tell her how much I liked her dress, that I had met her mother and daughter, that I loved her palace and that I thought she was absolutely wonderful. But there were still lots of other people waiting in the wings and I felt my wheelchair moving backwards to make way for them. But I had met the Queen. I had taken my curtain call.

The ceremony went on for another half hour or so as the other people received their various honours, but for me, time was frozen at that special moment when I shared the spotlight with the Queen of England. I shall always remember the warmth of her smile as she handed me that lovely memento of the occasion, the pink-ribboned, silver cross of the MBE.

Today, with little to do but remember, I see the medal and the photographs of me at Buckingham Palace as representing the climax to a long lifetime of ups and downs. They tell me that something of what I have done has been appreciated and no actress could ask for more.

Photoset, printed and bound in Great Britain by REDWOOD BURN LIMITED, Trowbridge, Wiltshire